FRAMING THE FALKLANDS WAR

Natio... and iden...

Edited by
JAMES AULICH

Open University Press
Milton Keynes · Philadelphia

For Alice and a better world

Open University Press
Celtic Court
22 Ballmoor
Buckingham
MK18 1XW

and
1900 Frost Road, Suite 101
Bristol, PA 19007, USA

First Published 1992

British Library Cataloguing-in-Publication Data

Framing the Falklands War: Nationhood, culture
and identity.
  I. Aulich, James
  306.0997

  ISBN 0−335−09684−0
  ISBN 0−335−09683−2 (pbk)

Library of Congress Cataloging-in-Publication Data

Framing and Falklands War/edited by James Aulich.
     p.   cm.
  "This book is a development of the exhibition 'The Falklands
factor' which took place at Manchester City Art Galleries . . .
1988/89"−Pref.
  Includes bibliographical references and index.
  ISBN 0-335-09684-0. − ISBN 0-335-09683-2 (pbk.)
  1. Falklands Islands War, 1982. 2. Falkland Islands War, 1982—Art
and the war. 3. Falkland Islands War, 1982−Literature and the war.
4. Falkland Islands War, 1982−Motion pictures and the war.
5. Falkland Islands War, 1982−Public opinion. 6. War in the press
−Falkland Islands. I. Aulich, James.
F3031.5.F72 1991
997'.11−dc20   91-20128 CIP

Typeset by Graphicraft Typesetters Limited, Hong Kong
Printed in Great Britain by Redwood Press, Melksham

Contents

List of Illustrations   v

List of Contributors   vii

Acknowledgements   viii

Foreword
Paul Greengrass   ix

Introduction
James Aulich   1

1   Touched with Glory: Heroes and Human Interest in the News
John Taylor   13

2   'There'll Always Be An England': The Falklands Conflict on Film
Jeffrey Walsh   33

3   Whose War is it Anyway? The Argentine Press during the South Atlantic Conflict
Nick Caistor   50

4   'We are All Falklanders Now': Art, War and National Identity
Tim Wilcox   58

5   Wildlife in the South Atlantic: Graphic Satire, Patriotism and the Fourth Estate
James Aulich   84

6   A Limited Engagement: Falklands Fictions and the English Novel
Nigel Leigh   117

7   'When the Seas are Empty, so are the Words': Representations of the Task Force
Robert Hamilton   129

Bibliography
Joanna Rose   140

Index   147

List of Illustrations

Fig. 1   Andy Robarts, *Memorial to HMS Sheffield* (1990)   4
Fig. 2   Adrian Brown, *40 Commando Marines Show-off Posters sent by The Sun, at Ajax Bay* (1982)   5
Fig. 3   Front page, *Daily Star*, 20 June 1990   25
Fig. 4   Simon Weston, who survived the destruction of *Sir Galahad*, appears on the cover of the *Radio Times* in 1989   27
Fig. 5   Sabát, *Carlos Gardel, Juan Domingo Perón y Leopoldo Fortunato Galtieri, Clarin*, 4 April 1982   53
Fig. 6   Linda Kitson, *Sheepsheds at Fitzroy – 2nd Battalion Scots Guards* (1982)   61
Fig. 7   Linda Kitson, *The Rudolf Steiner Hairdressing Salon, SS Canberra* (1982)   62
Fig. 8   Jock McFadyen, *With Singing Hearts . . . Throaty Roarings* (1983)   64
Fig. 9   Rosalind Furniss, *It's a Full Life in the Army* (1982)   66
Fig. 10   Michael Peel, *Rejoice, Rejoice II* (detail) (1982)   67
Fig. 11   Peter Kennard, *Falklands Medal* (1983)   68
Fig. 12   Michael Sandle, *Medal of Dishonour* (1986)   70
Fig. 13   Falklands Task Force crownmedal (advert)   71
Fig. 14   Michael Sandle, *Caput Mortuum: A Commentary* (1983)   72
Fig. 15   Graham Ashton, *Lifeboat, Ha!* (1983) and *Fasciol Fiasco* (1983)   73
Fig. 16   Paul Gough, *Deluge* (1987–88)   75
Fig. 17   Peter Archer, *Sgt. Ian McKay VC, Mount Longdon 11–12 June 1982* (1983)   77
Fig. 18   David Cobb, *The Canberra's Return to Southampton* (1982)   78
Fig. 19 and 20   Collages produced by servicemen during post-traumatic stress disorder therapy at the Royal Navy Psychiatric Hospital, Haslor   80
Fig. 21   Gerald Scarfe, 'We shall fight until the bitter compromise', *The Sunday Times*, 11 April 1982   86
Fig. 22   Bill Caldwell, 'We're expecting a big crowd later', *The Star*   87
Fig. 23   Keith Waite, '. . . and here is our first World Cup Football result . . . Argentina 79 Belgium 0', *Daily Mirror*, 15 June 1982   90

Fig. 24 Stanley Franklin, 'Ten ... Nine ... Eight ... Seven
         ... Six', *The Sun*, 30 April 1982   91
Fig. 25 Cummings, 'Prisoner in the dock! You are accused of
         giving a black eye to this skinhead when he mugged
         you!', *Sunday Express*, 8 May 1982   93
Fig. 26 Steve Bell, 'If ... This is really too bad, Kipling! Why
         are you engaged in this barefaced treachery??', *The
         Guardian*, 16 April 1982   93
Fig. 27 South Atlantic Souvenirs, 'Let's Go Over the Top
         with the Tories: 255 Reasons Not to Vote
         Conservative' (1982)   95
Fig. 28 Giles, 'But when the blast of war blows in our ears
         ... Stiffen the sinews, Summon up the blood ...
         Clear out the old air-raid shelter', *Sunday Express*,   96
         3 April 1982
Fig. 29 Les Gibbard, 'The price of sovereignty has been
         increased – OFFICIAL', *The Guardian*, 6 May 1982   99
Fig. 30 Zec, 'The Price of petrol has been increased by one
         penny – OFFICIAL', *Daily Mirror*, 1942   99
Fig. 31 Steve Bell, 'You know Kipling it's not every day your
         country wins a considerable victory ...', *The
         Guardian*, 24 June 1982   100
Fig. 32 Peter Brookes, cover design for *The Listener*,
         17 June 1982   101
Fig. 33 Martin Cleaver, *Dawn over the South Atlantic on
         board HMS Hermes*   101
Fig. 34 Nicholas Garland, 'Clear the Decks', *Daily Telegraph*,
         21 May 1982   103
Fig. 35 Nicholas Garland, 'Nothing except a battle lost can
         be half so melancholy as a battle won', *Daily
         Telegraph*, 5 May 1982   104
Fig. 36 David Hopkins, 'Let him go?', proof of cover for *The
         Economist*, 15–21 May 1982   106
Fig. 37 Lord Aberdeen restraining the British Lion, *Punch*,
         1854   107
Fig. 38 Les Gibbard, 'Whoops a little boob there fans! See
         The Sun stop the knockers tit for tat!', *The
         Guardian*, 10 May 1982   111
Fig. 39 Les Gibbard, 'Ssh, from you-know-where', *The
         Guardian*, 14 June 1982   112
Fig. 40 Cummings, 'I wish our all-conquering Field Marshal
         could liberate the British islands from the Union
         Junta!', *Sunday Express*, 26 June 1982   113

List of Contributors

James Aulich, Lecturer in the History of Art and Design, Manchester Polytechnic. Co-editor of *Vietnam Images: War and Representation* and co-organizer of the exhibition 'The Falklands Factor: Representations of a Conflict'.

Nick Caistor, talkswriter at the BBC World Service, former Latin American Researcher for *Index on Censorship*. Editor of *Contemporary Latin American Short Stories*, journalist and translator.

Robert Hamilton, Lecturer in History of Art and Design at Manchester Polytechnic, currently researching the roles of British photojournalists in the Vietnam War.

Nigel Leigh, assistant producer BBC TV's Documentary Features Department and author of *Radical Fictions and the Novels of Norman Mailer.*

Joanna Rose, Falklands Project research assistant, Manchester Polytechnic.

John Taylor, Senior Lecturer in History of Art at Wolverhampton Polytechnic. Author of *War/Photography. Realism in the British Press.* Series Editor for 'Studies in Photographic Culture', editor of *Ten-8* international photography magazine, exhibitions consultant for the National Museum of Photography, Film and Television.

Jeffrey Walsh, Lecturer in English Literature at Manchester Polytechnic and author of *American War Literature: 1914 to Vietnam* and *A Tribute to Wilfred Owen*; co-editor of *Tell Me Lies About Vietnam: Cultural Battles for the Meaning of the War* and *Vietnam Images: War and Representation.*

Tim Wilcox, Assistant Keeper, exhibitions, Manchester City Art Galleries, co-organizer of 'The Falklands Factor: Representations of a Conflict' and editor of *The Pursuit of the Real: British Figurative Painting from Sickert to Bacon.*

Acknowledgements

Books of this kind inevitably involve the inspiration, help and support of many people. I owe a spiritual debt to Jeffrey Walsh without whose work on Vietnam this Falklands project would never have been initiated. The book is a development of the exhibition 'The Falklands Factor', which took place at Manchester City Art Galleries during the winter of 1988–89 where Tim Wilcox was a vital and enthusiastic collaborator. The work was aided and abetted by the project assistant Joanna Rose and generously supported by Professor Diana Donald in the Department of History of Art and Design at Manchester Polytechnic and Howard Smith, Keeper of Exhibitions, Manchester City Art Galleries. I must thank Paul Greengrass and my editor Ray Cunningham for smoothing the path and credit the patience of friends. As always, to Lynn I owe the most.

Foreword

Paul Greengrass

'Do you forbid us to make the film?' I asked the Minister. 'Oh no, my dear fellow. After all, we are a democracy, aren't we? You know we can't forbid you to do anything. But don't make it, because everyone will be really cross, and the Old Man will be very cross, and you'll never get a knighthood.'

Thus the late Michael Powell describes in his memoirs *A Life in Movies* the classic confrontation between artist and politician over his 1943 subversive classic *The Life and Death of Colonel Blimp*. Powell's memoir proves that the British have always had cultural no-go areas. The Falklands War is one of those subjects today, like the recent history of Northern Ireland, and anything connected with espionage. They touch a raw nerve.

Part of the reason lies in the huge weight of symbolism attached to the Falklands War. It was a priceless opportunity for those who prosecuted it to lay the ghost of Suez – that haunting moment when Britain's Great Power pretensions were finally unmasked. Things would never be the same again.

John Osborne's *The Entertainer* captured the mood perfectly. The fading music hall turn Archie Rice tries to make a pathetic comeback against the backdrop of this national humiliation, as his son meets his death in the desert sands.

Suez symbolized the start of a growing tide in Britain towards iconoclastic freedoms of expression on stage, screen, television and journalism which reached fruition in the 1960s. But 25 years later they petered out. When the Falklands War happened it was proof, if proof were needed, that the tide had turned at last.

'We have,' Mrs Thatcher told the nation triumphantly at Cheltenham Racecourse, 'put the Great back into Great Britain!'

The war became a national exercise in myth making. This was not the grubby low-intensity reality of conflict in Ireland. This was war as we knew it from our childhood comics – Captain Hurricane charging machine gun posts single handed. It was like a film. We know, because we saw it on the telly. And of course, it was all over quickly. Most of all, we won.

There has been, I think, a conspiracy of sorts to bury the Falklands experience. Not a smoke filled room conspiracy, but a national conspiracy born of shame which prevents us from confronting the realities of that war, and the fact that, like a junkie, Britain took a lethal fix of jingoism and xenophobia in 1982.

But what was injected into the national bloodstream continues to swill around today. We went through a trip wire in 1982, and found out, or convinced ourselves, that war wasn't that bad. It could even be good for a nation. We repeated it again in 1991 in the Gulf. And the danger is that we may look back in another 25 years and say that the Falklands War was a kind of Suez in reverse – a great symbolic moment where the tide began to flow ever more swiftly towards easier wars, video nasty culture and diminished freedoms.

Already the signs are there. The years since 1982 have been ones of retreat – retreat from freedom of expression, retreat from standards of decency. You can see it in the tabloid press, you can see it in the attacks on journalism and drama, and in the Spycatcher Affair and, much more seriously, in the hounding of Salman Rushdie.

But it is not all gloom. The movement towards greater expansion of the priceless domain between the true and the real remains strong. It can be seen in the writing of Salman Rushdie and Julian Barnes, as it can in the films of Derek Jarman and Peter Greenaway. And there are some signs that the national myths erected at the time of the Falklands War are beginning to break down.

People remain troubled by the bellicosity of the language used during the Falklands War, and the grotesque symbolism with which it has all been imbued. People wonder what it says about Britain that we felt it necessary in the 1980s to consecrate our national revival in warfare and bloodshed. Surely, they think to themselves, there are other ways for a mature democracy to create heroes.

Other countries are content to create their national rhetoric on the back of a high quality football team, or an Olympic champion. But not us. There is a line of sorts, however loose, between the Paras yomping their way across the Falklands to the lager louts of today, laying waste to European cities in the name of football.

Bertolt Brecht summed up this internal unease in *Galileo*:

'Unhappy the land that has no heroes,' says Andrea.
'No,' replies Galileo, 'Unhappy the land that needs heroes.'

Introduction

James Aulich

It is tempting to begin this introduction with a quotation from David Harvey's (1989) *The Condition of Postmodernity*:

> The recognition that the production of images and of discourses is an important facet of activity that has to be analysed as part and parcel of the reproduction and transformation of any symbolic order. Aesthetic and cultural practices matter, and the conditions of their production deserve the closest attention.[1]

It is the intention of this collection of essays to investigate the area of aesthetic and cultural practices in the context of the recent history of the Falklands conflict. As a whole, the collection attempts to address the question: 'How did the conflict over the Falkland Islands attain the status of national crusade for the Argentinian and British peoples?' Or, in other words: 'How could the ideological consequences of the conflict be understood to outweigh historical significance to the extent that critics could express a sense of disproportion, feelings of distaste and observations of political expediency?' The conflict, as Anthony Barnett noted, was characterized by a curious air of unreality as the vacuum created by the absence of hard news, so assiduously controlled by the Ministry of Defence, filled with an almost neurotic assertion and identification of government, nation, monarchy, family and individual in a mosaic of verbal and visual imagery profoundly lacking in historical substance. The war, it seems, in the thrall of contemporary communications, disappeared in a haze of national hubris and undifferentiated diplomatic farce, domestic drama, imperial glory and real human heroism, all too often darkened by tragedy.

Briefly, in the spring of 1982 a war was fought between Britain and Argentina over the sovereignty of the Falkland Islands or the *Malvinas* as they are known in Argentina. General Leopoldo Galtieri, the leader of the military junta in Argentina, ordered the invasion on 2 April 1982 and rallied a national cause to his faltering military regime. In Britain, immersed in perennial domestic and political crisis, the occupation of the islands was widely perceived as a demeaning slight by a Third World nation towards a world power with a special relationship with the USA. In retaliation, the British Government with full parliamentary support put a large Task Force of ships and military units to sea in record time. The fleet sailed over 8000 miles to where the islands are situated off the coast of Argentina in the South Atlantic. The British forces advanced across windswept terrain to liberate the capital, Port Stanley, on 14 June 1982 where most of the 2000 inhabitants lived. On the way there were over 1000 British and over 2000 Argentinian casualties in just 33 days of fighting. After the defeat, General Galtieri's government collapsed. Subsequently, some members of the junta have been brought to trial. The democratic civilian government of Raul Alfonsin has been replaced by that of Eduardo Menem and talks have reopened with Britain in the certain belief that the future of the Falkland Islands must be renegotiated.

Since the conflict, events in Europe have made Britain's position appear more and more marginal as the cold war draws to its close and, inexorably, Europe moves towards economic and, perhaps, political unity. History has dispersed the triumphalist assertions of the last decade. And, it is increasingly clear that the political rhetoric of the 1980s was filled out with a symbolic vocabulary derived from particular and partial notions of history, nationhood, patriotism, sovereignty, democracy, monarchy, family and the individual. Notions, summed up, in part, by Margaret Thatcher when she said in October 1982, 'The spirit of the Falklands was the spirit of Britain at its best. It surprised the world that British patriotism was rediscovered in those spring days. But it was never lost.'[2] This fervent new age rhetoric evaded the issues of economic recession, high unemployment, unpopular government policies and personalities, but found concrete historical expression in the events of the Falklands conflict. It expresses a moral idea of England that is confident and steeped with evangelical fervour. As a result, a potent narrative developed which was cogent, pervasive and persuasive, despite the fact that it was built on the spurious foundations of partial understandings of national history and contemporary conditions. A veil of images aestheticized politics more thoroughly than at any time since the Second World War. Indeed, in the light of the acknowledged marginal long-term economic or strategic value of the Falkland Islands to British interests, the whole escapade seems truly quixotic. So powerful was the sense of national destiny, that following diplomatic ineptitude and intelligence failings, the British Government with a deeply unpopular Conservative majority under the premiership of Margaret Thatcher risked its political vision of renewal in a military gamble it believed it could not lose.

In retrospect, the Falklands crisis was more of a local symptom than a cause in the flux of late capitalism. On a rhetorical level, Thatcher had come to power on a raft of certainty manufactured from a nostalgic and rose-tinted view of Britain's historical role. The war gave this rhetoric of the New Right substance and in so doing gave it credibility in the popular imagination. Previously, the optimism of the white heat of Harold Wilson's technology had dissipated in the sink of post-industrial pessimism where for a great many people in this country and elsewhere the question of self-determination somehow simply seemed to be no longer on the agenda. Old certainties of industrial order based on the common sense of an honest day's pay for an honest day's work had been compromised by the new globalism of communications technology and international finance. Tradition and locality had succumbed to their instantaneous and destructive embrace. In this climate of disillusion certain readings of history could provide some sense of security. And here we find the invocation of the time of fate, myth and the Gods in the representation of the conflict. For the British and the Argentinian 'peoples', a discursive framework for the historical events of the war was secured around assumptions of racial, sporting and military superiority belonging to already established and safely predictable narratives of national pride. As this collection of essays demonstrates, their vocabularies are constructed in emblems and images to provide meanings coded within the terms of their production and consumption, shifting and slipping according to their constituencies. In the media, fine arts, drama, film, novel and the popular arts hierarchies privilege certain readings over others as we move from the explicitly political to the artistic, or, at the other end of the spectrum, the purely commercial. 'Britannia's Armada', for example, would have various, if not divergent emphases depending on the contexts of The South Atlantic Appeal Fund, the *Daily Telegraph* or *Private Eye*, for example.

Understandings of narratives like these are conditioned by their institutional organization and acquire layers of meaning in the course of their use in everyday life; some are authentic, others are contrived and all are constructed. They form part of a normative landscape whose substance bears comparison with the Afghan *baluch* or rug emblazoned with the emblems of modern warfare and resistance: the helicopter, the personnel carrier, the hand grenade and the AK-47 assault rifle. National myths have their existence in the weave of our lives through the agencies of the printed and broadcast media, publishing, education, museums, galleries and government. Such myths find expression in cultural products like the news broadcast, the documentary photograph, the cartoon, pulp literature and the poster which are commonplace, almost unnoticed elements in our essential environments. While others like fine art and perhaps film, television drama and the novel are privileged discursive practices. Each takes a place in, and competes for, our understandings of the world according to our individual backgrounds of race, gender, class, wealth and education. Some of these expressions are complex and are rooted in a sense of community and nation more subtle than many would allow. Andy Robarts' *Memorial to HMS Sheffield* (1990) (Fig. 1) erected in Barrow General Hospital, for example, is an elaborate and 'difficult' allegorical abstract sculpture with a high art pedigree, seemingly paradoxically commissioned by the people of Barrow-in-Furness. The commission was born of a profound

Fig. 1   Andy Robarts, *Memorial to HMS Sheffield* (1990), Barrow General Hospital, Partnership Arts Ltd, Hyde, Cheshire. (By kind permission of the artist.)

sense of loss and it commemorates the tragic fate of the *Sheffield* and the town's lifeblood working-class tradition of naval shipbuilding despite, and perhaps because of, the implicit irony in the commentary to the Vickers Film *HMS Sheffield*: 'With the hull of the *Sheffield* safely afloat the keel of a second Type 42 is swung into position on the vacant berth, this is the *Hercules*, the first of two Type 42s ordered from Vickers by the Argentine Navy.' Mediations of historical experience like these furnish the rooms of our conversations and house our (mis)understandings of the world.

In Britain, one national myth that was invoked effectively and frequently partook of a discourse of British Naval supremacy. It begins with Queen Elizabeth I and finds its apotheosis in the final victory over Fascism in the Second World War. This narrative provided a particularly potent set of symbols in representation of the fight against General Galtieri's military junta, regardless of the actual historical scale of the problem and, it seems, regardless of the inevitability of bloodshed once the myth had been invoked. There is no discursive space for negotia-

Fig. 2 Adrian Brown, *40 Commando Marines Show-off Posters sent by The Sun, at Ajax Bay* (1982). (By kind permission of the photographer.)

tion. Historical events are mediated and the public prepared for war, so that, at a time of crisis the present becomes meaningful within 'natural' orders. This early 1980s narrative of national pride, reliant on memories of Empire and two World Wars, can be partly characterized as Blimpish nostalgia. As Nick Caistor indicates, Argentina invoked a similar discourse of military invincibility by reference to the defeat of the British in Buenos Aires in the nineteenth century and the more recent and ruthless 'dirty war' against indigenous opposition groups (suitably demonized as Communist insurgents). In this context, it is tempting to suggest that part of the reason for the dramatic collapse of the Argentinian Government after the war was that there can be no regeneration for the vanquished because there is no available myth to accommodate defeat.

Evinced in Adrian Brown of 40 Commando's private photograph *Marines Show-off Posters sent by The Sun at Ajax Bay* (Fig. 2) taken during the campaign, are the arguments of John Taylor and Robert Hamilton. They show how the popular newspapers, in their reporting

of departures and arrivals of the members of the Task Force, constructed a rite-of-passage from the adolescent national province of the
football terrace to the adult world of the international stage. The young
men of the armed forces as representatives of the nation, individually
and collectively, found regeneration through violence: bloodied through
the heroism of war they returned to the promise of sexual fulfilment
and, as the narrative's necessary corollary, a mature role for the country
in the affairs of the world. Might becomes right and the Great is put
back into Britain in a narrative of national moral superiority and true
patriotism whose legacy in the behaviour of the British abroad is still
with us as a measure of its potency. Jeff Walsh and Tim Wilcox discuss
the portrayal of the failure of this myth and its consequences within
what Herbert Marcuse called the humane marginality of art.

More often the 'natural' imperial order of Britain's world role was
re-established in a constructed spectacle of a heroic and charismatic
moral code easily found in popular fiction – as Nigel Leigh argues. But
John Taylor, on the other hand, demonstrates how in the media the
tragedy of Colonel H. Jones' death becomes an immortal role to be
emulated. Hierarchical structures and propaganda replaced rationality
and knowledge more clearly than at any time in recent history. Destiny
of an almost divine quality was seen to unite the people in the will of
the state and nation to promote a most uncharacteristic John Bullish
deference to authority. The power of the myth of blood and soil implicit
in the paramount claims of the islanders as British citizens (a status
which they were about to be denied under the Nationality Act), the
claims of sovereignty, and its defence as an act of sublime national
achievement, provided a sense of permanence concealed within the
historical cause of anti-Fascism. The declaration 'We are all Falklanders
now!', quoted by Tim Wilcox, established a unity between the people
and the land through a tradition of English Romanticism and con-
veniently avoided social divisions inscribed in the problems of class,
privilege and deprivation. Stable mythologies supported paradoxical
claims for nation and community against those of a dominant ideology
of rootless, opportunistic, individual enterprise.

Significantly, the sense of triumphalism continued well into the run
up to the 1983 General Election as the Prime Minister exploited military success for political ends. The Victory Parade on 12 October 1982
was the largest ever staged in London. It stretched from the Honourable
Artillery Company to Guildhall and the salute was taken at Mansion
House. As Michael Cockerell indicates it served the necessary cathartic
function of ascribing a form of immortality on those who had died and
allayed wider anxieties held by the population with regard to mortality,
it was also a spectacular affirmation of Margaret Thatcher's temporary
incarnation as monarch and national figurehead. A phenomenon, as I
hope to show, that cartoonists exploited throughout the campaign to
various effect. The parade's imperial ceremonies and memories reached

back at least as far as ancient Rome and gave it the dual function of contextualizing the victory among the greater achievements of Western civilization while at the same time attributing Margaret Thatcher regal status. A tendency signalled when she recycled the words of Queen Victoria used by Winston Churchill on the wall of his Second World War bunker in Whitehall: 'We are not interested in the possibilities of defeat, they do not exist.' The unconscious conflation of national interest with an individual personality ironically aped General Galtieri's position in Argentina as Nick Caistor illustrates. Unsurprisingly, the *Daily Mirror* noted on its centre pages 'there was something missing ... the Queen' and duly reported Thatcher's regal gestures; even the *Daily Telegraph* addressed the event within the terms of 'The War we could have Lost' and criticized Thatcher for her overblown rhetoric when she described the British forces as not only the most professional but the *bravest*. Not even at the height of the Second World War had Churchill made such claims.

Prime ministerial excess and Royal absence was compensated in the press by the raising of Henry VIII's doomed flagship the *Mary Rose*. The *Daily Mirror* registered 'Royal Joy' as the *Daily Telegraph* reported: 'The great day of patriotic fervour began when the ribs of the *Mary Rose* emerged.' And contrasted it with the 'Royal Rage' of the Falklands War hero Prince Andrew, photographed with Koo Stark on Mustique, forced to 'hijack' an aeroplane to engender his 'great escape' in appropriately dashing mode.[3] It is tempting to read this royal escapade as a parallel narrative or national projection mediated through the press. Genuine human emotions of grief and remembrance at the Victory Parade; or, of lust or affection on Mustique are symbolized in representatives of the monarchy as embodiments of the 'true nation'. But both are compromised by the 'vulgar display' of a common woman: Thatcher, on the one hand, and Koo Stark, on the other. A reading partly confirmed by Keith Waite's depiction of Thatcher as a drum majorette striding over the caption 'Who did you think would be leading it?'[4] However, her self-appointed role progressed undiminished. At the beginning of 1983, when Thatcher secretly visited the islands this regal role was reinforced, as David Watt of *The Times* observed: 'The hushed reverential tones adopted by the tv announcers, the expensive seconds of tv time spent establishing pictorial frames for her pictorial tableaux, the constant references to her troops, all proclaim this is a royal visit.'[5]

So, despite some equivocation and distaste in the dominant media (*The Financial Times*, for example, ignored the Victory Parade and most papers reported it in terms of those who had recovered from traumatic wounds, or from the point of view of the grief of relatives of those who had died), the overall effect was to further the identification of a charismatic leader with the cause of the nation. The parade provided a representation through which certain spatial and temporal practices might function as part of a mechanism of social control on behalf of a particularly authoritarian and unyielding government. This 'Resolute Approach', as indicated by Michael Cockerell, prolonged the uncomfortable aesthetic identification of party politics and national interest to the 1983 Conservative Party Conference when in front of a backdrop resembling a grey battleship the widow of Colonel H. Jones took a seat on the platform alongside Thatcher, while 'Rule Britannia!' was reserved for the leader's triumphal entry for the Final Conference Speech.[6]

A sustaining emblem for the territorial claims of both sides of the conflict was the map. Peter J. Beck has made the observation that by law in Argentina maps have to show the Malvinas as part of the national entity, permeating an imaginary annexation of the islands through school textbooks, atlases and stamps, for example.[7] In a widely published Argentinian cartoon, the Argentinian World Cup mascot carries under his arm the map of the islands. In Britain, the map is handed by Thatcher to the Queen in a cartoon by Stanley Franklin in *The Sun*; or it is used as an aid to explain Britain's historical claims and to speculate on military strategy in the printed and broadcast media. Like the Victory Parade, it has a semiotic value which produces a 'natural' order to determine practice and in turn reinforce social order (reproduction). Furthermore, in the face of the pink of the Empire, an uncivilized Argentina could only put up a primitive and pagan resistance; the journalist Gordon Brook-Shepherd wrote (simultaneously identifying the enemy in the fifth column of Scargill, Foot, Benn *et al.*): 'Yet though it is not on the Dark continent we have failed, but here at home' where in the face of 'a spirit of national regeneration ... the message of Goose Green proving the only message against them ... we had to wait two years after Mafeking for final victory against the Boers.'[8] In this way the representation of the campaign becomes identified with notions of 'white man's burden' and all that that invokes. Particularly, in the realms of national moral responsibility which are linked with state authority and remain divorced from the claims of the population at large.

The stability represented in the map can only be transgressed by force of arms and violation will guarantee retaliation. These maps not only reified territory and its inhabitants as property to be held and owned, but also provided an imaginative space that fixed certain collective memories which were put into motion by the Argentinian and British governments like the 'secret agents of aspiring powers'.[9] A process which is replete with irony since few people had heard of the islands when the conflict began and the media helped fill the gap with appropriate geographical and strategic maps of the South Atlantic; significantly, a set of Falkland Islands stamps issued in September 1982 sported the map used by the BBC during the conflict. As David Harvey has observed, Heidegger had pointed out that:

Space contains compressed time. That is what space is for: 'Is this the foundation for collective memory, for all those manifestations of place-bound nostalgias that infect our images of the country and the city, of region, milieu and locality, of neighbourhood and community? And if it is true that time is memorialised not as flow, but as memory of experienced places and spaces, then history must indeed give way to poetry, time to space, as the fundamental material of social expression. The spatial image then asserts an important power over history.'[10]

Something, according to Tim Wilcox, Surgeon Commander O'Connell might attest to in relation to his patients undergoing treatment for post-traumatic stress disorder and the pervasive, if directed, use of the map of the Falklands in art therapy. And something the cartoonist Ralph Steadman and the television producer and director Peter Kosminsky implicitly recognized in their dissent from the dominant view. The former interpreted the map of the islands as two fly-infested lamb chops for the cover of the *New Statesman* on 14 May 1982 and the latter presented it as a blood stain on a white sheet for the opening sequences of the Yorkshire Television Production *The Falklands War: The Untold Story* (1987).

This is as true for photographs as maps, particularly in the case of Tom Smith's *Welcoming Cup of Tea at San Carlos Settlement*. Smith was annoyed to discover that of all the many photographs he sent back, this picture of a paratrooper sharing a cup of tea with some of the islanders over a garden fence was the most widely published. The image set the action in the naturalized conditions of a domesticated countryside and in so doing established the commonsense terms of a pastoral and classless 'Britishness' that draws upon memories of a romantic tradition. Similar use of the landscape is made in establishing shots in Emeric Pressburger and Michael Powell's 1943 film *The Life and Death of Colonel Blimp* to authenticate an ancestral and almost aristocratic pedigree of an old order; while in the BBC TV drama, *Tumbledown* (1988), the landscape encompasses the lush wooded green hills of the officer class; and in the film *Resurrected* (1989), the rugged topography and 'dark satanic mills' of the working-class Lancashire/Yorkshire border stands in for the life of the squaddie. Yet, each is emphatically British.

As Jeffrey Walsh indicates, the neo-romantic certainties of this pastoralism are questioned in all three films. Colonel Blimp returns to the remnants of a disappearing aristocratic world. His certain belief that a fair, clean and hard fight could only prove right is might in the face of the treachery and inhumanity of the enemy, is challenged by the subterfuge of his own younger and inferior officers. For Captain Lawrence in *Tumbledown* it is the home of a leisured middle-class hypocrisy of which he is the victim, while for Guardsman Philip Williams in *Resur-*

rected it acts as the foil for an impossible masculinity from which he must escape. In the news media, however, 'Blimpism' succeeds as it could not in fiction: the enemy was quickly established as villainous, prepared to use napalm, just as the Germans had used gas in the First World War; and, whose decadent officers relaxed in relative luxury while the conscripts froze in inadequate shelters and whom they shot in the knees or feet to prevent them fleeing the remorseless British advance. Unlike reportage, film is granted the 'truth of fiction' where 'Blimpishness' has little validity in the face of cheating, traumatic injury and institutional insensitivity.

Likewise, the traditional hierarchical framework of Martin Cleaver's widely published photograph *Training on Hermes* establishes the individual's relationship with advanced technology and military efficiency in a way that the private, unpublished photographs of the violated bodies of the dead taken by individual members of the Armed Forces cannot. The former conforms not only to the natural order of the news photograph but is also determined by notions of good taste, fear of offence and interests of national morale. As John Taylor, Robert Hamilton, Tim Wilcox and myself show, these determinations are reinforced by the traditional forms characteristic of the cartoon, the day-by-day calendars of the national press and the continuous stream of new brides, recent widows and thankful reunions. These stable structures of space and time did not, or more likely were formally unsuited, to address or question conventional meanings, as Nigel Leigh cogently argues in relation to the conventional structure of the novel. Unlike, perhaps, more self-consciously avant-garde forms such as those discussed by Tim Wilcox, or the 'art house' movie styles of Richard Eyre or Paul Greengrass with their elaborate symbolism and non-sequential narratives. Or, the fragmentary montage styles of Ralph Steadman, Peter Kennard (Fig. 11) or Michael Peel (Fig. 10) and the parallel narratives of Steve Bell (Figs 25 and 30) or Raymond Briggs. Or, indeed, the private photographs and art therapy of individual servicemen. The observation finds its historical metaphor in the fact it took three days for videos of World Cup matches to reach the Task Force and three weeks for hard TV film to reach London. This meant the contemporary representation of the Task Force was situated firmly in mythological or historical time, the slow speed of its reporting more appropriate to a previous imperial age. While the Task Force's dispatch and reliance on advanced communications actually placed it firmly in the instantaneous present of the satellite age. Such are the significances of the structures of space and time.

By various means conflicts can, in part, be manufactured in signs rather than the specificities of history. Indeed, the Argentinian commentators Cardozo, Kirschbaum and van der Koy, authors of *Falklands: The Secret Plot* (1983) and Michael Charlton the British author of *The Little Platoon: Diplomacy and the Falklands Dispute* (1989) have argued that the war had more to do with mutual misunderstanding and diplomatic ineptitude than anything else. Neither nation at the beginning of the dispute, or even at its height, suffered any serious external threat as Britain had during the dark days of the Second World War, yet both sides generated a tide of romantic nationalism to act out a charade of certainty, sustaining spiritual values and common purpose. In this country, the representation of the quest for victory in the Falklands projected nostalgia for common values among a highly mobile, self-seeking and materialistic society of individuals in a mirage of national and natural superiority. The military achievements and political fallout of the Falklands campaign, are produced, constructed and marketed in a culture industry which manufactures representations of the present as the pastiche of a partially illusory past. It is a form of heritage which becomes a clear mark of social identity by means of the various consumer constituencies belonging to cultural institutions in society.

The intention of this volume is to examine through the analysis of particular cultural productions some of the processes whereby the individual viewer unconsciously incorporates particular external ideas of nationhood, for example, as 'universal' and 'natural' imperatives which inform his or her essential being to produce collective manifestations of nationalism in varying degrees. Identity is found to a certain extent in the cultural productions which make up part of everyday life and they constitute a discourse of competing narratives where the individual subject is, in part, constructed. Thus constituted, the state is able not merely to collect taxes but manipulate our psyches and control our bodies: to throw us into a fatal conflict with fellow human beings that had as its justification a loss or gain of national pride. Under these conditions community exists on the level of the nation, family on the level of the monarchy, individual on the level of the subject. As Michael Foucault has noted:

> This form of power applies itself to immediate everyday life which categorises the individual, marks him by his own individuality, attaches him to his identity, imposes a law of truth upon him which he must recognise and which others have to recognise in him. It is a form of power which makes individuals subjects. There are two meanings to the word 'subject': subject to someone else by control and dependence; and tied to his own identity by a conscience or self-knowledge. Both meanings suggest a form of power which subjugates and makes subject to.[11]

Notes

1 Harvey, D. (1989). *The Condition of Postmodernity*. Oxford, Basil Blackwell, p. 355.

2 Margaret Thatcher, quoted in the *Sunday Express*, 10 October 1982, p. 1.

3 *Daily Mirror*, 12 October 1982, pp. 1–3.

4 *Daily Mirror*, 11 October 1982, p. 1.

5 Quoted by Cockerell, M. (1989). *Live from Number 10: The Inside Story of Prime Ministers and Television*. London, Faber and Faber, p. 269.

6 Ibid., p. 284.

7 'Argentina's philatelic annexation of the Falkland Islands', *History Today*, Vol. 33, No. 2, 1983, pp. 39–44.

8 Brook-Shepherd, G. (1982). 'The pep in patriotism', *Sunday Telegraph*, 11 October, p. 18.

9 Bachelard, quoted in Harvey, op. cit., note 1, p. 217.

10 Ibid.

11 Foucault, M. (1984). 'The subject and power'. In B. Wallis (ed.), *Art After Modernism: Rethinking Representation*. New York, New Museum of Contemporary Art, p. 419.

| 1 | Touched with Glory: Heroes and Human Interest in the News

John Taylor

The Battle for the Story

The Falklands campaign makes a simple story because the events follow each other in a connected series: the Argentines invade the islands; the British send a fleet to recover them; the opposing nations clash at sea; the British land and fight battles which they swiftly win; they return home to a quayside celebration. The story is enriched by two domestic events which attach to the military victory: the rail union ASLEF abandon their threatened strike (workers take their cue from the professionalism of Other Ranks, and do their duty); Princess Diana gives birth to a boy (fulfilling in a timely manner all that was expected of her by providing a king for the twenty-first century).

This simple story was not completed until the ending was known. However, the narrative had still to unfold, and the national press played its part in writing its progress. The Falklands campaign was a military event not only in history: it was an event which was written, and was always in the process of being written, even as it happened. It has 'often been noted', in the words of a theorist of the media, Denis McQuail, that there is a 'tendency for news reports to be cast in the form of a narrative, with principal and minor actors, connected sequence, heroes and villains, beginning, middle and end, signalling of dramatic turns [and] a reliance on familiar plots'.[1]

In the aftermath of war, the Select Committee of the Ministry of Defence sat in judgement on the telling of stories. The politicians summoned people from the military and the media, but the Committee was not formed to respond to gripes against the extent and machinery of censorship. Its purpose was to clarify the rules of censorship and the place of the media in military planning for future wars and the future framing of morale on the home front.[2]

The Committee was concerned less with the diversity of news reporting than with a single potential – the power of realism. Television and newspapers use different types of realism, although there are correspondences. In television news the filmed image moves and, if shot in extreme conditions (or by an amateur), may be jerky and indistinct: the voice-over or journalist-in-frame gives authority to what we see and take to be an authentic representation of things actually happening.[3] In the newspapers, it is photography which is realistic. There is no development in time, but the image offers a confirmation of existence, a seemingly transparent window-on-the-world.

This unproblematic belief about film and photography is both innocent and resilient. Yet the causative link between the pre-photographic or filmic referent and the sign guarantees 'nothing at the level of meaning'. As the photographic historian, John Tagg, says, 'The photograph is not a magical "emanation" but a material product of a material apparatus set to work in specific contexts, by specific forces, for more or less defined purposes.'[4] The meanings of representations emerge from and are confined by *practices*.

The Committee's interest in realism, however, stemmed from a simple belief in the authority of television and photographic images *in themselves*. The danger was not only the journalists' use of imagery in the context of news organizations, but that mass communication produces direct action.[5] Like the Task Force and Ministry of Defence (MoD) censors who decided what should be broadcast or printed, the Committee had a simple belief in 'media effects' and the idea that people will act as a result of what they see in pictures. The Task Force commanders and MoD limited the access of film crews and photographers to the battlefields because they were afraid of pictorial realism and its effects. Television in the war zone showing dead or badly wounded British servicemen 'would be distressing to families and would be upsetting to morale.'[6] They were afraid that the realism of pictures could overwhelm the still-censored stories. Then the authorities could not easily seal the gap between their preferred view of the war which had been accepted by journalists but contradicted by film.

For the same reason, still photography was carefully controlled. The Task Force sailed in April with no facilities for transmitting black-and-white photographs. Some 6 weeks later, the two press photographers had been able to return just two batches of pictures to London. This material was shipped to Ascension; because there was reported to be no darkroom on the island to develop the prints for wiring, the film had to be flown to Britain.[7] Only three batches of photographs were received at the Press Association in London before the establishment of the beach-head in May. Then two ships with wiring terminals were brought forward for the first landings. One photojournalist went ashore at this stage, but the other 'had no landing facility for approximately twelve days after the initial assault'.[8] In all, the number of photographs transmitted was only 202.[9]

In its memorandum to the Select Committee, *The Scotsman* noted that many photographs were sent back with 'apparently unequal speed': 'as the conflict wore on, bad news was taking far longer to come out than good news, presumably in the belief that the effect would be dulled'.[10] *The Scotsman* claimed 'that it wasn't simply chance that the celebrated picture of San Carlos villagers offering a marine a cup of tea achieved such instant currency',[11] while the photograph of *Antelope* exploding[12] suffered a delay of 3 weeks.[13] It seemed that the war was being deliberately 'sanitised'.[14] In his interview before the Committee, the Defence Correspondent of the Press Association, Bob Hutchinson, said that journalists were told by the Prime Minister's Press Office that 'Number 10 felt that enough bad news pictures had come out'.[15]

Bad news is a staple of the newspaper industry, and some journalists felt the government had made a tactical error by presenting the war as unbelievably clean. In their view, high morale was related to balance in the reportage of war, a balance that was expected to be discernibly objective and believable. The editor of *The Guardian*, Peter Preston, said to see no pictures of casualties at all invited suspicion of laundering the facts, or a cover-up for political reasons.[16]

The journalists were quick to blame the government for its handling of the media and left out of the account their own everyday practice. Press censorship is never a simple matter of outside direction from government and the media practise self-censoring. Photographs of the dead were taken, and did reach the Press Association (PA). One of the press photographers, Martin Cleaver, said there were pictures of dead bodies in the PA library which were released by the Ministry, but newspaper editors decided not to use them.[17]

This reveals a congruence of interests to which the commander of the land forces, General Sir Jeremy Moore, made reference. Commenting on the adverse effects of realism upon morale, he said the absence of 'unpleasant' scenes came from 'the good taste of our journalists'.[18] From the official perspective, the authorities and the media appeared to agree about what was acceptable during a national crisis. Again from the official perspective, they appeared to be joined in this convergence by the news-hungry audience itself, which was supposed to have applied pressure from below and ensured a patriotic consensus on clean news or no news at all. The Defence Committee believed journalists avoided the disturbing effects of shocking film and photographs because of their own 'good taste' *and* their professional ability to meet the expectations of the newspaper audience. The Committee said the public also had 'good taste', which 'will ultimately impose standards of taste and decency on the media if any elements are tempted to concentrate on the more lurid and distressing imagery of war'.[19]

Storytelling in the Press

The Defence Committee treated the media as united by realism and was interested chiefly in the threat to morale. It paid no attention to the main use of realism in both broadcasting and newspapers, where pictures deepen the truth-value of the verbal reports. Photographic realism authenticates storytelling in the printed news because experience cannot be described, or in the attempt the words fail. Experience is then said to 'beggar description', and the deficient account shored up by photographs. These are accepted as 'the thing itself', forgetting that photographs are also representations. By combining words and pictures, the newspapers pretend to close the gap between experience and language.

Even though the press is not a single homogeneous unit, and different sectors prefer different styles of address for their imagined audiences, they all use realism in reportage: its confirmation of existence anchors their different modes of address, presenting the illusion of a complete map of the real. Before looking at the types of story that are presented as real (and which are all accompanied in the originals by photographs), a very brief description must be given of differences in the market.

There are several ways in which newspapers compete with each other. The major difference is between the tabloids and broadsheets. The tabloids are roughly 'down-market' in terms of the social aspiration and economic power of readers, whereas the broadsheets are roughly 'up-market'. This suggests that *Daily Telegraph* readers have more in common with *Guardian* readers than with readers of *The Sun*. Other distinctions must include readers' age-profile and gender: for instance, the *Daily Star* and *The Sun* address young males, whereas the *Daily Mail* and the *Daily Express* address older readers and women.

Political differences are most marked among the broadsheets. For instance, *The Guardian* was less enthusiastic about the campaign than the *Daily Telegraph*. When Rear Admiral Sandy Woodward said the recapture of South Georgia was 'the appetiser', the *Daily Telegraph* reported the story under the headline 'Heavy Punch Coming Up' (27 April), but it did not give coverage to his revised opinion two days later. On the other hand, *The Guardian* said, 'Admiral changes his "walkover" tune', and 'Force chief talks of long and bloody fight' (29 April). *The Guardian* also carried a fuller report of the Admiral's controversial remarks: 'This is the run up to the big match, which in my view should be a walkover.'

The competition for readers sometimes refers to standards of reporting. Within the tabloid market, the *Daily Mirror* (8 May) turned on *The Sun* for its trivializing and inaccurate coverage of the crisis, calling its rival the 'Harlot of Fleet Street'. The broadsheet press also attacked the 'lower end' of the market for its dubious professional standards. The political columnist Simon Jenkins, writing in *The Times* (10 May), remarked upon the gap which had opened up between the jingoism of the press and the moderation of the public as expressed in opinion polls and radio phone-ins. He said, 'For the past five weeks, the bulk of the British media has been representing the Falkland crisis in a stereotype born of Hollywood out of the Second World War. As if on some archaic autopilot, the tabloid press has cartwheeled across the sky with "Give 'Em Hell", "In We Go!", "Stick It Up Your Junta" and "Victory". After "Gotcha" ', he observed, the 'glorious escapade began to dissolve.'[20]

This style of address did not always signal an unusual gap between the journalists and the readers. On the contrary, the address was usually in keeping with past practice. This was plain in *The Sun*'s and *Daily Star*'s interweaving of sex and war. Sexual life floods the news, and the Task Force became a sex Force. Whereas in the *Daily Express* (13 April), it was sufficient to signal the stereotypes of gender division in stories about the 'woman who waits' and 'men of war', in papers whose imagined audience is young males the routine of picturing women as sex objects was transferred to the war zone. These papers followed their normal (sexist) practice of weaving stories around bare breasts, sexual slang and *double entendres*. For instance, *The Sun* placed 'Invincible garters' on nude models who were then described as 'shipshape Bristol fashion' in 'nautical naughties' (16 April). Another staple of the whole industry, favoured especially in relation to sex, is alliterative language: 'QE2' and 'cutie' was irresistible to *The Sun*, which reported (12 June) on the sexual allure of soldiers on board the troop ship in 'Sexy capers on the ocean rave! QE2 cuties fall for heroes'.

The *Daily Mirror* avoided models but reported women who bared their breasts. On 13 May, it pictured a half-naked woman who bared herself at the quayside with the caption, 'A big lift for our boys'. But what had been a report in the *Daily Mirror*, next day was turned into a feature by the *Daily Star*. It drew the same half-naked woman away from news into the category of erotic entertainment, persuading her to pose as a '*Daily Star* bird' (14 May). All these 'birds' were generously given over to Prince Andrew because of his famed sexual prowess (28 May). As the *Daily Mirror* reported (4 June), he doubled as a famous military and sexual 'Action Man'. All the tabloids reported on the Prince as a decoy for the Exocet missile, though only the *Daily Star* gave this explicit sexual connotations, with 'Decoy Andrew, "I lured exocet" ' (19 June). The tabloids used sex as a unifying principle, levelling men in the enterprise, banishing differences of rank or fortune. Sex, in its stereotypical forms, subsumed the whole project in pin-up coyness, or dressed it in the familiar and comfortable humour of the seaside postcard.

As we see here, the press chose a narrow range of conventional relations between the language and practice of sex and war. Other usual crossovers in imagery is of taking, spending, pushing back, pinning down and disarming. The more thrilling and dangerous interactions of sex, death and war were unexplored. The soldier-hero fuels his body armour with his own blood; the ability to pump it and even in the end to spill it signifies his manhood. The difference between blood-as-fuel and blood-sacrifice is critical for individual soldiers, but less so for the body of the victorious army which moves on the hot fuel of survivors. These experiences of soldiering were turned into press stories, but expressed in the already established, ordinary language and pictures of the news industry.

Human Interest

The general conditions of storytelling set by the censors or the self-censoring practices of the news industry were not the main determinants of war coverage; nor was consumer sovereignty (to the extent that it exists) a major factor. Most important of all was the news industry's reliance upon the human interest story. This category concerns the birth and death, marriage and divorce, health, wealth and habits of the great, and especially of Royalty, the aristocracy, film stars and athletes. The same details about ordinary individuals must have a special element of the sad, the comic or the bizarre to make them interesting.[21] The category has important ideological significance. It is widespread, and so it becomes the rhetorical small-change through which it is possible to achieve meaning, and through which people are enrolled in the imaginary unity of the real. In the words of sociologists of the industry, 'human interest' is 'not simply a neutral window on a multifaceted and diverse world but embodies a particular way of seeing the world'.[22] This they describe as a rejection of the possibility of basic structural inequalities in favour of the random and non-historical forces of 'luck, fate and chance, within a given, naturalised world'.

The position of the human interest story within its everyday practice helps to place the newspaper industry close to the official version of events. There is a congruence of interests between the government, the army and the newspapers in this matter. Human interest stories are the most widely read in both the tabloids and broadsheets. Their appeal carries across the differences between men and women, young and old, middle- and working-class. Stories written from within this framework can transform overtly political news. As a result, awkward questions about the (historical) social relations of power remain unasked, and history is replaced by whatever can be felt, such as 'natural revulsion' or 'common sense'.

Human interest is an ordinary factor of the news story along with other shared and structural characteristics of newspapers. Although they are remade every day, they are drawn over the ghost of the previous day's product. Again, there is cohesion within each day's issue. All are shaped so that readers experience no sense of loss in moving from the front page to the back: news does not diminish and eventually disappear. On the contrary, newspapers sharply define their segments and each offers the possibility of renewed interest in newsworthiness and entertainment.

The sections of the paper are different: there is home and business news, overseas news, feature articles, leaders, letters, arts and women's pages, sports pages and advertisements. Yet each section offers only a different mix of the twin poles of misery and its opposite. Twinning is crucial, since the world of the press is Manichaean: the strength of one is checked only by the power of the other, good news heralding consumption, with bad news casting a shadow over all delights, threatening the withdrawal of pleasure for ever. On hard news pages, there are more problems than solutions, while a complete reversal takes place in the fabulous worlds of advertisements and fantasies of entertainment. The papers show us the perversity, fragility and chaos of existence, and temper this knowledge with comfort and excitement in store. They are threaded through with hope and dismay, with life and pleasure ceasing for some and at the same time endlessly renewed for the present readership, the present survivors. Permissions to enjoy and warnings of mortality are commonly reduced to simple polarities. A news story is whatever gladdens the heart or saddens it, whatever is heart-warming or heart-rending. The sense of one depends upon the proximity of the other – hence the pairing of words like 'triumph' and 'tragedy'. They are linked but not held in permanent opposition to each other. Indeed, one may turn into its opposite, victory become defeat and vice versa. Whatever the result (and we are forewarned that it may be unexpected), the story ends in triumph or tragedy.

When the Falklands campaign was still unfolding, there could be no ending; with the outcome uncertain and so much at stake there was only room to repeat the purpose of the Task Force, and the moral worth of the enterprise. This overriding purpose, stemming from abstractions such as sovereignty or beliefs about the British way of life, had to be clarified for readers on a daily basis, brought home or made to seem real and immediate. This moral posture could be satisfied in stories with endings, which represented the issues in miniature, which were the epitome or essence of the whole campaign.

Fate and the Family

Baulked as they were by the censorship or lack of hard news from the Task Force, the press had considerable resources in their daily practice of telling and retelling stories. Not knowing the outcome, everyone was (metaphorically) on the edge of their seats. The psychic tension of a drawn-out affair was relieved in smaller stories that were completed in the day. The favoured stories told of the flow and ebb of life, fate and magic, triumph and tragedy. Not that the press are monolithic or deterministic in their use of fate in human affairs: the broadsheets analyse politics and economics, for instance, more than the tabloids, whose reliance upon fate is concomitantly greater. Yet the papers share the tendency to place people at the mercy of powerful forces. These are often natural phenomena such as the catastrophes of floods and quakes; 'tragedies' relating to the natural world and released by human agency, such as droughts and pollution; or conditions of social life as different as revolutions and corporate businesses. The reader is given a kaleidoscope of events, or (less entertainingly) events in a staccato procession which seems merely reactive. People struggle against natural forces of incomprehensible purpose, and against human forces that are out of control, or at least not in the control of readers. News, through the repetition of mischance and escape, drives home the random and unforgiving, elemental forces of fate.

To place the action of individuals at the heart of human affairs is a commonplace in Western society. In any war, individuals give up, or have taken away from them, the potential for choice. They become subject to the dictates of others who release the technological surprise with weapons of unusual or unknown levels of destruction which may 'seal their fate'. In the Task Force, the random destructive effects of both fate and technology were supposedly tempered by the soldiers' professionalism, of which intelligence is a crucial part. Once they had the enemy in sight, they expected to destroy it, passing destiny into the control of the Task Force. As Admiral Woodward's notion of a 'walkover' suggested, things were supposedly arranged so the death-lots would be drawn by the enemy. When reality broke in, sense had to be made of British deaths.

The nature of the conflict was to split families up in a way that was unusual even for the armed services. For enlisted men the spectre of death is ever-present and being in the Task Force moved it from near to proximate. In the newspapers, the saving and breaking of families was the hope and the danger of the war. They used the opportunity to publish photographs which exemplified each wish and fear. On 8 April, the *Daily Star* published the photograph of a wife who waited for news of her husband who was a prisoner of war; on 19 April he was freed and the *Daily Star* printed a photograph of the wife talking to her husband by phone; on 21 April the two were pictured kissing, with the caption, 'Home to the arms of love'. Heart-warming stories of the reunion of families were newsworthy, and recurred throughout the war but particularly on 8 June when the survivors of the *Atlantic Conveyor* arrived in England. The headline in the *Daily Express* was 'Daddy's Home', in *The Times*, 'Family reunion' and in the *Daily Mail*, 'Home are the Heroes'. The pleasure of homecoming was never pure, since many were lost. In the *Daily Express* story, this was indicated by photographs of the 'tearful reunion for survivors of lost cargo ship'. In the *Daily Mail*, the 'heroes' had come 'home' but with their 'tales of horror'. 'Hugs of delight' for the 'men who came back', now 'holding the baby again', were set against a portrait of Captain North, skipper of the cargo ship, captioned with the stark words, 'he vanished'. The destruction of the family was always immanent, and could be represented simply by drawing banal family snapshots into the newsnet. The *Daily Express* published 'The last portrait of a dead hero' – the man, his wife and baby son (1 June); the *Daily Mirror* published a photograph of a woman holding the portrait of her husband and called it 'missing presumed dead' (7 May).

However, the national newspapers are not an almanac: they do not report the routine deaths of people. It was generally insufficient for men to have died in the Falklands for their photograph or pictures of their families to register in the news. A denotation of the newsworthy is the 'special', or out-of-the-ordinary. Although irony is a commonplace in newsworthiness, it is not always found in the manner of death or in premonitions. On 26 April, the *Daily Mirror* reported the death of a man who had said, 'It's just a job.... It's what I've been trained for.' In this case, the irony was not unusually savage. Equally ordinary were his interests – he had been a 'footballer, keep-fit fanatic and devoted husband'. What drew him into the newsnet was the *moment* of his death, being the first to die: that made him special and the piece was captioned 'Last Call for Britain's First Victim'.

To be the first or last to die, or in some other way to die in cruel circumstances, or to leave the bereaved in unusually bitter or ironical straits was to be newsworthy. These moments of death were reported with similar or same family snapshots in the tabloids and broadsheets. They included untimely ends, such as the one described in the *Daily Star* (18 June) as 'Last Battle of Hero Jason', at 17 years fated to be the youngest victim. Bitter moments for survivors stemmed from the special circumstances surrounding the fate of husbands. The *Daily Mirror* (2 June) said, 'The Widow, Wendy, 17, mourns husband of three weeks', and the *Daily Telegraph* said, 'Bride of 17 mourns her husband'. Another heart-breaking case was the couple fated to have no married life at all: the headline in *The Sun* (10 June) was 'Grief of war widow', the '8 hour bride', and in *The Times*, 'Helicopter crash leaves one-day bride a widow'. A different twist was the woman fated to be a new 'teenage bride', and to learn of the deaths of her husband and his best man: the headline in the *Daily Mail* (15 June) was 'Just married: Debbie flanked by two teenage Guardsman soon to die', and in *The Guardian*, 'Pride and pain of brides made widows at Bluff Cove'. Bitterness and irony combined in the story, reported in *The Sun* and *The Guardian* (16 June), of a family who 'rejoiced' at the announcement of the cease-fire minutes before they were told of their son's death. In another case, *The Guardian* reported a 'double blow' (16 June), and *The Sun* called it the 'Double-death heartbreak of tragic sisters', telling how two women learnt that both their husbands were dead, the irony being in one travelling to comfort the other but discovering her own loss on returning home.

The convergence of details makes these incidents heart-rending, because they are more ironical and cruel than is usual. Each story is sufficient in itself, but the variations on the theme meet another standard test of news: the story which is the-same-but-worse. Clearly, incidents in the world are not organized to worsen progressively. It is fortuitous if worse examples follow on day by day, but since there is no absolute scale and only the urge to hear of novel twists to the basic formula, the category is fulfilled by the simple heaping up of horrors or the addition of refinements. All the above examples are versions of the-same-but-worse. The coherence of this type of news around families can be seen in a story reported in the *Daily Mirror* and *The Times* (1 May) that is terrible but peripheral to the Task Force: a soldier returned home after training to find his wife had been murdered. The suffering was removed from the campaign; the act was criminal; the event was newsworthy chiefly because of an ironical twist — with the death visited upon the unexpected person.

Within days, there were deaths among the waiting military forces. On 2 May, the *General Belgrano* was sunk and 2 days later the *Sheffield* was hit by a missile, reported in the *Daily Express* (5 May) as 'Revenge of the Argentines'. The *Mirror* headline (6 May) reflected hope as well as horror: it said, 'Don't worry, mum, we'll knock the living daylights out of the Argies', reported almost as a dream against the awful reality. Death had fallen upon the best of professional groups. The destruction of the *Sheffield* showed that control could be easily lost, that the enemy could strike back. The lack of intelligence, not knowing or misreading the movements of the enemy, could not be described as a fault among commanders in the Task Force so much as mishap that brushed aside the defences and aspirations of even the righteous.

Fate is blind, and reasoning over the deaths of comrades remains the gift of survivors — with most value accruing to the words of close relatives. They could make or unmake the sense of the war. The father of a dead pilot made sense of it by tying together the abstraction of patriotism with the pleasure of professionalism. He was widely reported (6 May) as saying 'I am proud to have a son who died doing the job he loved for the country he loved.' In contrast, and not so widely reported, were the views of those relatives who could find no reason for it. For instance, when a cook died, his mother was quoted in the *Daily Mirror* (6 May) as saying he had not joined the Navy to die for something as 'wasteful' as this.

The dissenting voice of an awkward relative was largely ignored, and it seems families rarely resisted the official version of their son's death. They preferred to accept the idea of heroic death 'in action'. Unusually, and therefore newsworthy, one family pursued the authorities for years, eventually forcing them to reveal the actual circumstances of death. In the process they stripped away the patriotic rhetoric, exposing the raw waste. In 1988, *The Guardian* said 'an inquest verdict that an army helicopter pilot died "as a result of enemy action" ... was quashed by the High Court yesterday after the judges heard how the aircraft was shot down in error by a Royal Navy destroyer'.[23] This family placed historical circumstance above personal comfort. They demanded the authorities admit error rather than use the convenient euphemism.

Making sense of the war, from the official perspective, involved a different weighting of fact and value. Whereas for some individuals, fate might explain why a particular person had died, the rhetoric of arms could not allow fate-as-death to settle upon the Task Force in any simple way: death had to be transmuted into glory. Moreover, the progress and outcome of the war could not be left to fate-as-chance: the Force must take control of its destiny through professional soldiering and impose itself upon the Argentines. In contrast to the controlling British, the enemy were made subject to fate. They were destined to be defeated because of the illegality of their cause. Yet the defeat of this criminal government and misled army, rather like the fascists of Hitler's Germany, could not happen automatically: it required acts of great daring by the British. Their power lay not in brute force alone but in spiritual force, holding the enemy in thrall and so captivating it as a prelude to defeat.

Dead Hero

The spirit of a force is its heroes and every story has them. This process is fully worked through in the press reports of the most famous of the 255 British dead, Lieutenant Colonel Herbert 'H' Jones. Leading his men in an attack at Goose Green, he was in advance of an enemy position and was shot down from behind, becoming the highest ranking officer to be killed on land.[24] His death was newsworthy because of his high military rank, his class (Eton and Sandhurst) and his bravery. The headline in the *Daily Star* (31 May) latched onto the family's shortened form of his Christian name in their headline 'H is for Hero'. To be known as H was fortuitous, and all the papers except the *Daily Telegraph* used it immediately. The name suggests the elemental, giving the colonel a firm outline – something which, coincidentially, has its graphic equivalent in the square-jawed heroes of Empire and comic book stories. In these stories and in reports of military action, the death of a hero must be avenged, and the loss of a hero demands unusual gains. Here, part of the compensation was in prisoners: the *Sunday People* said, 'Colonel H is killed . . . and we take 900 Argie prisoners' (30 May), which next day in the *Daily Star* became 'the incredible story of Colonel H and the 600 paras who captured 1,400 Argentines'. *The Guardian* carried the same figures without presenting them as unbelievable: indeed, it reported an officer saying, 'The victory is entirely his. It was his plan that worked' (31 May).

However, a hero's life for great numbers of prisoners is not a fair exchange: the loss is incalculable and so the gain must be unnumbered.

The papers used the mundane idea of paying a price, but linked it with the valued act of bravery. The *Sunday People's* headline said, 'Red Berets' hero Pays Price of Courage' (30 May): the value which meets the 'price of courage' is invested in the Colonel himself, which he then 'spends' to buy the victory. In the *Daily Mirror* headline, 'The Price of Victory' (31 May), the value is exacted from the Colonel by an ideal but demanding future. 'Courage' is the fuel of 'victory'. The terms are more spirited than the measured advantage of captured arms and ground. It is this rhetoric, rather then the numbered captives, which signals the transformation of the Colonel from the category of alive-but-invisible to that of dead-but-larger-than-life.

The heroism of Colonel H was made legible in the move from being named to being honoured. *The Sun* translated him across symbolic thresholds to burial in a 'Field of Glory', and the ordinary became its opposite (1 June). Dead soldier-heroes are normally made complicit in this. Their real and involuntary deaths in battle are displaced by a symbolic and active choice of death marking the field of glory. The soldier is typically said to have 'fallen', or 'laid down his life' as a 'sacrifice'. The idea of sacrifice makes sense of individual courage since it spurs the group on to victory. The nobility of sacrifice and its Christian associations are transferred to the survivors, who attest to this and show their gratitude in remembering 'fallen' soldiers.

Paradoxically, the dead soldier-hero is never at rest. He is constantly revived in memory. In the case of Colonel H, a remembrance service held in the village church was widely reported, with a front page photograph in *The Guardian* (10 June). He was one of only two soldiers to receive the Victoria Cross. He continues to 'stand in' for the patriotism of 1982: in June 1990, the *Daily Star* (self-styled 'paper fit for heroes') ran a front-page article on the Colonel. There was a large photograph of his (unnamed) widow who was reported to have said, 'I plant a tree to his memory every year'. In her 'moving story' on the inside pages, the caption read, 'Place for memories: Colonel H's widow Sara in the garden where she plants a tree each year on the anniversary of her husband's death in the Falklands'. This place is described in the text as 'The corner of England that is forever H', a variation on the lines 'That there's some corner of a foreign field/That is for ever England ...' from Rupert Brooke's poem *The Soldier*. The significance rests in the determined link with the First World War – the last time that the language used to describe soldier-heroes could evoke that nuance in English patriotic sentiment without risk of an admixture of irony (Fig. 3).

Framing the story of the death of heroes is not the prerogative of newspapers, or even their speciality, and could not be sustained without a national rhetoric of remembrance. This extends most completely to the various types of memorials to the dead of the First World War which were built in churches, civic centres, public parks and village

DAILY Star
THE PAPER THAT GIVES IT TO YOU STRAIGHT

WEDNESDAY, JUNE 20, 1990   22p (23p Cls)

A paper fit for heroes

'I plant a tree to his memory every year'

Col 'H' Jones' widow opens her heart to the Daily Star

READ HER MOVING STORY TODAY ON PAGES 14 & 23

Royal ladies in red

WELL A-HEAD: Di and Fergie both ended up in the red in the Royal Ascot fashion stakes yesterday. Ascot Thrills — Page 5 Pictures FRANK BARRETT

FAITH HEALER SNUBS ENGLAND

DAILY Star Exclusive

THE STRUGGLING England World Cup squad is so desperate that it has called in a FAITH HEALER.

But miracle worker Olga

By IAN TRUEMAN and BOB DRISCOLL

Stringfellow has rejected the request — because she hates manager Bobby Robson.

"He wouldn't have the

decency to pick up the phone and ask me himself — because we don't like each other."

A senior member of the England squad called in 67 year old Olga to treat injured skipper Bryan Robson. She has helped him before and club officials thought she could cure his

Turn to Page 2, Col 3

Fig. 3 Front page, *Daily Star*, 20 June 1990. (Express Newspapers plc.)

greens. Those who died overseas were returned, symbolically, to their locality, their names were inscribed on monuments, enduring in the annual Remembrance Day services and among the visitors to the sites.

The war-time death of soldier-heroes is never enough for the press. The newsnet will scoop up courageous soldiering, though papers usually reject elegy in representing the death of soldiers and concentrate upon the destruction of families and the creation of grieving widows. The case of Colonel H is no exception. In the *Daily Mirror* he was described as a 'soldier', but also as a 'family man' (31 May). In addition to his military and social rank, the Colonel was newsworthy *because* he was a family man. Ideally, the man in his absence will be matched by an equivalent but womanly presence, and Mrs Jones is herself a woman of social rank and fortitude. *The Sun*, under the headline 'My Hero', used a photograph of Sara Jones and H on holiday, whereas the broadsheets chose a photograph of the family at Buckingham Palace in 1981 when he received the OBE. Photographs from happy times are uncanny, placing readers in the privileged position of playgoers who already know or quickly learn what is withheld from the characters – their fate. Similarly, the photograph shows us the man who is lost, the loss of that loving or familial bond, making strange the possibility of happiness, making readers conscious of its fragility or transience. Ironically (and irony can be an important part of a story if it is sufficiently bitter), Colonel Jones was already known to the press, having threatened to 'sue everyone' because of the premature announcement of the fall of Goose Green.[25] In this case, the press made nothing of the irony.

The Wounded Hero

Not all heroes of spiritual force are dead ones. In telling the story of the Falklands campaign, of the 777 British wounded, Simon Weston is the most famous. He was badly burned when *Sir Galahad* was bombed at Bluff Cove. At the time he was not singled out, but later became famous when the BBC followed his progress of healing and rehabilitation. Three films were released: *Simon's War* in 1983, *Simon's Peace* in 1985 and *Simon's Triumph* in 1989. In April that year, his face appeared on the front cover of the *Radio Times*, and the story on the inside pages reviewed the earlier films. *Simon's War* had shown 'a young man forced to come to terms with wrecked hands and a wrecked face'. *Simon's Peace* had, if anything, 'deepened' the earlier 'vision' of anger and despair. It showed how the 'carefree, good natured young Welsh Guardsman was discharged by the army, had nothing to do, and fell into deep depression'. By 1989, Simon Weston had moved, according to the BBC, through 'war' and 'peace' to a 'personal victory'. He was now working and looking forward to the future, and was reported to have said, 'I just want things to turn out right' (Fig. 4).

The real passage of Simon Weston, as an historical being, from war

Fig. 4   Simon Weston, who survived the destruction of *Sir Galahad*, appears on the cover of the *Radio Times* in 1989. The caption says, 'I'm Simon Weston, see, not the Phantom of the Opera.' (Photograph by Nick Hedges.)

to peace to triumph fitted the shape of the Falklands War. That was a military campaign fought and won by British forces and, with peace restored, ending in the triumphal return of the fleet. The stories of the Guardsman and the campaign are parallel, but this has more to do with the shapes of stories than with historical events. In the endings of stories we learn what they mean; in stories of both personal and national significance we want to know if 'things turn out right'.

Making things turn out right is a process common to storytelling wherever it is found, in novels, films, private memories and public histories. It is also a process common in dreams, myths and fables. Indeed, the kinds of information which we call fact, fiction, history and myth constantly interact. Sometimes they are difficult to separate from each other, and can always be understood at various levels. Hence the Simon Weston story is fact and fiction. It has meaning at the level of an individual personal history, a life to be lived every day, and at the level of symbolism where it becomes part of a collective memory or national history.

The three BBC films on Simon Weston not only told a story about the Welshman, but they told it in a particular context. Although the Simon Weston story and the story of the Falklands campaign had the same outcome, they unfolded in different times. This is more important than their unfolding over different time-scales: the Falklands campaign was peculiar to 1982, but the Simon Weston story was played out against the backdrop of storytelling in the BBC from 1982 to 1989, years which proved to be critical for the position of broadcasting (and towards the end of the decade increasingly so for the press). During these years the government sought to influence in new ways the conditions in which stories were made, the general assumptions that underpinned the practice of the media and the details of particular stories. This is to suggest no more than a general background for the films, certainly not to hint at interference by government or cynical manipulation of the story by the BBC on behalf of the government. Nevertheless, in more politically sensitive areas than the Falklands, the government did wish to effect broadcasting. To understand this, broadcasting should not be treated in isolation, but placed in the wider political scene.

From 1982 to 1985, the Conservative Government were triumphant in securing their official perspective against the resistance of individuals and institutions. Here are some examples:

1 In May 1982, following the Panorama programme *Can We Avoid War?*, the Conservative Party's backbench Media Committee criticized the BBC for its lack of patriotism.[26]

2 In December 1982, the Ministry of Defence was vindicated by its watchdog Select Committee for the way it 'handled the media', and sometimes misinformed the public in the name of national security.

3 In April 1983, a BBC play, *The Falklands Factor*, was cut by 2½ minutes because the Corporation said it might have caused distress to

the families of soldiers. The author, Don Shaw, called it political censorship and pointed to the forthcoming General Election that June.[27]

4 In March 1984, the government successfully prosecuted Sarah Tisdall, a clerical officer at the Foreign Office, under the Official Secrets Act for leaking (in 1983) the Secretary of Defence's plans to introduce Cruise missiles to Greenham Common.[28]

5 In July 1985, Mrs Thatcher, the Prime Minister, called for the 'oxygen of publicity' to be denied terrorists, and the Home Secretary successfully persuaded the Governors of the BBC to press Alasdair Milne, then Director-General of the Corporation, into withdrawing its programme on Loyalists and Republicans in the *Real Lives* series, called *At the Edge of the Union*.[29]

These victories were followed by two signal defeats. In 1985, the government unsuccessfully prosecuted Clive Ponting, a senior official at the Ministry of Defence. He had released to a Labour Member of Parliament two memoranda he had been asked to write on the sinking of the *General Belgrano*: one gave the full circumstances of this incident and the other outlined what the public would learn, thereby misleading Parliament.[30]

The second defeat was more protracted, involving many gagging writs and court cases from 1986–88 against Peter Wright, the former MI5 Security Service agent, for publishing his memoirs, *Spycatcher*. He claimed that the head of MI5 had been a probable Soviet spy and that MI5 had been involved in secret plots to destabilize the reputation of the British Labour Party.[31]

These short-term defeats had longer-term implications because the government changed the law, placing secrecy above the public good.[32] They placed controls upon whistleblowers through the new Official Secrets Act, the Civil Service code of conduct and the Contempt of Court Act.[33]

From 1986 to 1989, at the same time it suffered these legal setbacks, the government continued to exert pressure on the BBC:

6 In September 1986, Conservative MPs attacked the Corporation over its 'drama-documentary' series, *The Monocled Mutineer*, which dealt with a British Army mutiny in the First World War, and which they considered suffered from left-wing distortion.[34]

7 The next month, Conservative Central Office (in a weak analysis which the professionals were able to discredit but which none the less received wide publicity) charged the BBC with biased coverage of the American raid on Libya.[35]

8 In January 1987, the Board of Governors induced the BBC to ban the *Zircon* film, which revealed the existence and costs of a spy satellite until then unknown to Parliament; Marmaduke Hussey, Chairman of the Governors, asked Alasdair Milne to resign.[36]

9 In August 1988, following the Ballygawley bomb which killed eight British soldiers, the government introduced a ban on radio and television coverage of those who 'support violence'.[37]

The struggles between the government and the broadcasters, in which the government always won in the end, are the context for the three films on Simon Weston. From 1982 to 1985, the government had great authority, but there were uncertainties. These were paralleled by the despair of Simon Weston's story. By 1989, however, the situation appeared more settled. The broadcasting authorities had been brought closer to the official perspective by internal changes to their governance and management.

At the same time as these changes were taking place, the convergence of opinion on the campaign came about for entirely different reasons. By the time Simon Weston was 'triumphant', the Falklands conflict had shrunk in newsworthiness. It was by then firmly in the past, bedded down in history, a brief but glorious chapter in Arms. The film *Simon's Triumph* was entirely appropriate to the wider political-media context and to the current view of the Falklands campaign itself. *Simon's Triumph* is part of that historicizing process in which retelling the story of a distant campaign fits present requirements. This is possible because the war was long ago and therefore the responsibility of others. Moreover, the Falklands campaign can be reinstated (in the language of journalism) as a 'triumph over tragedy', which was the title of the article in the *Radio Times*. The personal history was grafted onto the history of the whole campaign, summing it up and locating its symbolic meaning in the shift from misery to exultation. The problematic of individual action and responsibility in historical moments of great complexity was swept aside for a simple and reassuring solution: personal tragedy in warfare is the harbinger of national triumph. The sacrifice of Armed Forces ensures the continuing and undisturbed condition of civil society. The three films on Simon Weston's progress converged with the assessment of the campaign over the same period.

The message is the conventional 'happy' resolution to all kinds of stories, including fairytales and films, and is a favourite device in accounting for the past. Whole wars can be reduced to simple oppositions between good and evil, and to simple narrative forms using 'cause and effect' as the engine of change and explanation. Taking it all in at a glance, and knowing the glorious outcome, alters the perspective on defeats and local disasters. In winning the war it is permissible to lose battles, which in the victor's history sometimes vanish or more often become *cause célèbre*. The American historian Barbara Tuchman, speaking with some distaste, said, 'No nation has ever produced a military history of such verbal nobility as the British. Retreat or advance, win or lose, blunder or bravery, murderous folly or unyielding resolution, all emerge alike clothed in dignity and touched with glory.'[38]

Nothing, however, simply emerges: it is always produced by people in given conditions for more or less conscious purposes. The Falklands campaign is no exception, existing in the newspapers in a region untouched by censorship, in language and pictures shaped by ordinary practice into a diversion, a daily story to warm the heart or break it.

Notes

1 McQuail, D. (1987). *Mass Communication Theory*. London, Sage, p. 206.
2 House of Commons Defence Committee (December 1982). *The Handling of Press and Public Information During the Falklands Conflict*. Volumes *HC 17-I* and *HC 17-II*. The first volume contains the *Report* and the second the evidence of witnesses.
3 See, for instance, Fiske, J. and Hartley, J. (1978). *Reading Television*. London, Methuen; Hartley, J. (1982). *Understanding News*. London, Methuen.
4 Tagg, J. (1988). *The Burden of Representation: Essays on Photographies and Histories*. London, Macmillan, p. 3.
5 See, for instance, McQuail, D. (1977). 'The influence and effects of mass media'. In J. Curran, M. Gurevitch and J. Woollacott (eds), *Mass Communication and Society*. London, Edward Arnold in Association with The Open University Press, pp. 70–94.
6 Op. cit., note 2, *HC 17-II*, QQ. 1900–1904.
7 Nicholson-Lord, D. (1982). 'Ministry wakes up to propaganda war', *The Times*, 14 May.
8 Op. cit., note 2, *HC 17-II*, p. 308.
9 Op. cit., note 2, *HC 17-I*, p. xxxviii and *HC-17-II*, p. 7.
10 Op. cit., note 2, *HC 17-I*, p. xliii and *HC 17-II*, p. 117.
11 *Daily Express*, 25 May 1982.
12 *Daily Mirror*, 26 May 1982.
13 Op. cit., note 2, *HC 17-I*, p. xxxviii and *HC 17-II*, Q. 1230.
14 Op. cit., note 2, *HC 17-II*, p. 118.
15 Ibid., Q. 1230.
16 Ibid., Q. 1346.
17 Morrison, D. E. and Tumber, H. (1988). *Journalists at War: The Dynamics of News Reporting During the Falklands Conflict*. London, Sage, p. 182.
18 Op. cit., note 2, *HC 17-II*, Q. 1211.
19 Op. cit., note 2, *HC 17-I*, p. xvi.
20 Jenkins, S. (1982). 'When soldiers play journalists and journalists play at soldiers', *The Times*, 10 May.
21 For a description of 'human interest', see *The Tom Harrisson Mass Observation Archives: Mass Observation File Reports 1937–49*. No. 126, Report on the Press, May 1940, para. 1.1.
22 Curran, J., Douglas, A. and Whannel, G. (1980). 'The political economy of the human interest story'. In A. Smith (ed.), *Newspapers and Democracy: International Essays on a Changing Medium*. Cambridge, Mass., MIT Press, p. 306.
23 'Falklands death verdict quashed', *The Guardian*, 18 February 1988. See

also 'Briton died in missile attack by Royal Navy', 'Mother wins six year battle to reverse verdict on death of son in Falklands conflict', *The Independent*, 20 October 1988.

24 The full citation for Colonel Jones' Victoria Cross is in *The Times*, 11 October 1982.

25 Op. cit., note 2, *HC 17-II*, Q. 168.

26 See Glasgow University Media Group (1985). *War and Peace News*. Milton Keynes, Open University Press.

27 Wenham, B. (1988). 'Whose standards?', *Index on Censorship*, No. 8, p. 19.

28 Campbell, D., 'Paradoxes of secrecy', *Index on Censorship*, No. 8, p. 18.

29 Protheroe, A. (1986). 'The broadcaster's greatest hazard is fear', *Index on Censorship*, No. 1, p. 17.

30 Op. cit., note 28, p. 18.

31 Op. cit., note 29, p. 11.

32 Norton-Taylor, R. (1990). 'The Official Secrets Act', *Index on Censorship*, No. 6, pp. 2–3.

33 Ibid.

34 Editorial (1987). 'BBC under fire', *Index on Censorship*, No. 3, p. 7.

35 For a transcript of the newscasts, the Conservative Central Office analysis and the point-by-point response from the BBC, see *Index on Censorship*, No. 3, 1987, passim.

36 See, for example, 'The knock on the door in the night – Secret society', *New Statesman*, 6 February 1987, passim.

37 See Bonham-Carter, M. (1989). 'Broadcasting and terrorism', *Index on Censorship*, No. 2, pp. 7–8, 32–33.

38 Tuchman, B. (1971). *Stilwell and the American Experience in China 1911–1945*. London, Macmillan, p. 557.

I **2** I 'There'll Always Be An England': The Falklands Conflict on Film

Jeffrey Walsh

In concluding his influential study, *One Man's Falklands* (1982), Tam Dalyell prayed that history would not repeat itself: 'The best way in which Britain can do honour to the young lives that were lost and to our wounded and dreadfully maimed service men who will never be the same again – is to learn a lesson from the events of 1982 and make sure that such a situation is never repeated.'[1] By a profound irony, the lessons of 1982 *have* been learned, but in the opposite way to that which Dalyell intended.

American presidents have not been slow to learn the propaganda value of similar ruthless strikes against dictators, as events in Grenada, Libya and Panama have demonstrated. In the British media, conventional wisdom now is that Vietnam was an 'unfortunate' war, messy, costly and dragging on for far too long, while the Falklands operation offers a model for new style campaigns, allowing 'surgical' action that can 'take out' a tyrant without too much bloodshed. Observers of media presentation on the Gulf crisis have deplored this bellicose attitude.[2] Nigel Fountain, for example, argued that 'tabloids have used language that would have put any fourth year bully in the shade. Calls have been made for the razing of the Iraqi capital, and the possible use of nuclear weapons has been celebrated rather than condemned.'[3] A study of both the tabloids and quality press, together with television news items, corroborates Fountain's point. A familiar occurrence on current affairs programmes during the Gulf crisis was to see retired generals or weapons experts dramatizing war scenarios with the assistance of models and computerized graphics. In such war games, the Falklands was frequently referred to as a signifier of military prowess and triumph, an index of how it should be done.

Another interesting strand of rhetoric regarding the Gulf was recurrent reference to the Second World War, especially in the need to avoid repeating the policy of appeasement. Fortuitously for journalists, the fiftieth anniversary of the Battle of Britain was being celebrated concurrently, and so metaphors of victory against an evil aggressor came easily to hand. The media commonly linked the Gulf crisis, the Falklands, Vietnam and the fight against Hitler in this way as legitimation for the actions of Bush and Thatcher in defending 'Western values' against aggression. Historical differences are thus facilely elided in the spurious pursuit of newsworthy stories. It is understandable that war artists and writers feel the need to counter such historical misconceptions.

In representing the Falklands campaign, this issue of misleading stereotyping was addressed by Paul Greengrass, the director of *Resurrected* (1988), who admits to the influence on him of mythical British war films such as *Reach for the Sky* (1956), *The Dam Busters* (1954) and *In Which We Serve* (1942).[4] During a scene in Greengrass' film, *Reach for the Sky* is being televised, incongruously in a ward where Falklands veterans lie gravely wounded: the irony of Kenneth More's words, when he breezily wishes for yet more involvement in combat, is thus compounded. As this incident suggests, the inheritance and tradition of earlier British war films is a useful starting place for any analysis of filmic narratives of the South Atlantic conflict in 1982. This chapter begins by considering two of the Rank Organization's classic war films, Noel Coward's *In Which We Serve*, probably the most influential of all British war films, and one of its many imitators, Anthony Asquith's *We Dive at Dawn* (1943). Both films will be examined in the context of later developments. As the chapter proceeds, the major films narrating the Falklands operation and its social impact will be measured against these earlier, seminal representations.

Noel Coward and David Lean's British war film, *In Which We Serve*, opens with an epigraph that sets its tone: 'This film is dedicated to the Royal Navy "whereon the good providences of God, the wealth, safety and strength of the kingdom chiefly depend".' As the film's title infers, its narrative dignifies the ideals of service to sovereign and country under the protection of Christian values. At key moments in the story, Captain E. V. Kinross, played by Noel Coward, leads prayers, and there is also a loyal toast to King George made by the officers. *In Which We Serve* recounts the experiences of the crew of a destroyer. *HMS Torrin*, from its launch to the occasion of its sinking during the Battle of Crete with the loss of over half of its company. Its trajectory is one of spiritual victory arising from apparent defeat. The film's plot centres on the experience of three representative British couples: the ship's Captain and his wife, Alix: Ordinary Seaman Blake (John Mills) and his fiancée, later wife, Freda; and Chief Petty Officer Hardy (Bernard Miles) and his wife. The latter, Mrs Hardy, is killed in the Blitz just before Freda symbolically gives birth. In essence, the film cuts between the war zone and and events back in Blighty: it is organized retrospectively and structured around the ship's company.

The key moments of *In Which We Serve* encapsulate what we may call the responsible actions of the good father. The film concludes with its most moving scene when Captain Kinross – a character said to be based on Lord Mountbatten – shakes hands in simple ritual with his shipmates and surrogate sons. His words, 'No one will fail to do his duty to the very end', reverberate throughout the film. Kinross fulfils his obligations of leadership down to the minutest detail, writing to the families of wounded sailors, endlessly comforting his men and taking professional care of them. Like the King, the nation's revered and selfless father, his role is also sanctioned by older ties and traditions. This is apparent in the closing words of the film when he promotes the image of a future united nation: 'There will always be other ships, and men to sail in them.' Kinross is the living embodiment of ritualized Englishness, sure, stable, confident. His sons, the *Torrin*'s crew, perform feats of endurance, carry shells to the limits of their strength and, showing their gentler, more feminine side, respond to the German POWs with decency. They are without exception family-orientated men who treat their womenfolk with courtesy and genuine affection. The ideology of caring masculinity is resoundingly praised.

A central scene from *In Which We Serve* flashes back to Dunkirk, and pays homage to the fortitude and dignity of the British Expeditionary Force (BEF) in their darkest hour. Such an attitude characterizes the epic pattern of the whole film, which celebrates the famed Dunkirk spirit, epitomized in popular culture by such songs as 'Roll Out The Barrel' or 'Run Rabbit'. The lyrics of 'There'll Always Be an England' or the sentimental love ditty, 'If You Were the Only Girl In the World', also imply the pervasiveness of accepted national values, especially respect for women and country. Kinross has been shaped by the public school ethos of understatement and public service: he revealingly speaks of his ship, the *Torrin*, as demonstrating 'beautiful manners'; he seeks to create 'a happy and efficient ship' and, on hearing of acts of valour shown by the crew of a sister ship, says characteristically: 'I'd give my eye teeth for a show like that.' When he is shipwrecked, after being hit by enemy shells and is eventually rescued, one of his men expresses concern about his welfare. Kinross laconically replies 'I like a swim before breakfast.' His character, shaped by leadership and hierarchical culture, illustrates that, in 1943, the ideology of Englishness remains dominant and intact. Against an enemy said to be intent on world domination, all the British services are shown as united in opposition because, as one sailor suggests, 'The whole of civilisation is trembling on the edge of an abyss.' This thematic superiority of 'English' values is reiterated in minor ways too, as when Chief Petty Officer Blake declares his faith in the Daimler and Rolls because 'You can't touch a good old conservative British make' of car. He dismisses American models as ostentatious.

Gender and class are unproblematical in Coward and Lean's academy award winning film. Women are centrally situated at the heart of the narrative; Celia Johnson, Kay Walsh and Joyce Carey are co-heroines accorded representative status. The men are defined in relation to their wives or girlfriends, and the womenfolk comfortably accept their inevitable subordination to their rival, the *Torrin*. In a famous scene, Celia Johnson gracefully submits to the superior power of the ship in her husband's affections. *In Which We Serve* celebrates marriage, and underpins the woman's clear supportive domestic role: there are frequent shots, for example, of women knitting or presiding over meals. Class unity is also focused through familiar metaphors. Ordinary Seaman Blake is devoted to Captain Kinross: the wealthy Mrs Kinross reciprocates by being civil and friendly to his fiancée. Freda. There is no semblance of class antagonism portrayed, although cultural difference is clearly witnessed, for example, when the Kinross family eat grouse served up by a maid in uniform. The ship's officers, who speak in impeccable accents and are exceedingly well groomed, always behave politely and considerately towards the lower ranks.

In Which We Serve, a film produced during wartime, thus understandably articulates images of a unified and resilient nation, where both men and women, officers and ordinary seamen, work towards a common purpose. The film does not show throughout its entirety a black face: otherness is symbolized only by the German POWs who are essentially of the same ethnic family as ourselves. The contrast with a later film depicting a racist, post-Falklands, Thatcherite Britain, *For Queen and Country* (1989), which is discussed later in this essay, could not be greater. Coward and Lean's movie, perhaps the greatest war film of its generation, has stood the test of time because it constructed many of the most significant narrative patterns and attitudes later evident within the genre. It was a seminal work.

Anthony Asquith's *We Dive at Dawn* is a film of lesser artistic quality, which is nevertheless interesting because it shows how many of the constituents of *In Which We Serve* are popularized. The narrative of Asquith's film is a simple adventure story whereby the submarine *Sea Tiger* undergoes a successful mission to destroy the German battleship *Brandenburg*. In essence, the plot emphasizes the valour of the submariners and their adaptability in combat. When *Sea Tiger* runs out of fuel, one of its crew, Hobson, played woodenly by Eric Portman, carries out a daring raid on a German outpost, which is situated on an offshore Danish island. This incident provides the excuse for an implausible hand-to-hand fight showing the exceptional daring of the British raiding party. The Germans are stereotypically represented as being rather ineffective and ponderous. In these respects, the content of *We Dive At Dawn* is clichéd and recognizable later in a plethora of succeeding war movies of the action and adventure kind. What is interesting, though, in Asquith's film, is its assured ideological understructure.

We Dive At Dawn echoes *In Which We Serve* in its depiction of the good father, in this case Captain Taylor, played by John Mills. Taylor, as does Captain Kinross, takes responsibility for his men's lives, and is keenly interested in their domestic problems. He is willing to give advice and also to concern himself trying to solve their emotional difficulties. This aspect of masculinist caring is evident in the story of Hobson whose unsteady marriage is ultimately resolved with a happy outcome. The crew of *Sea Tiger* contains no subversives or malcontents; they symbolize unity of purpose and fierce resolution to defend King and country. The film, lacking the emotional range or artistic complexity of *In Which We Serve*, similarly shares with the earlier, innovative film a controlling attitude that somehow war is a game which we play in more civilized fashion and, therefore, deserve to win. Images of a cheerful seafaring group, devoted to families and wives, symbolize a united island race at war, determined to triumph over adversity. Such a narrative, varied and inflected, provided the staple plot for a series of following British war pictures. The values and ideals informing the struggle against Nazi oppression were rarely called into question: nowhere could there be detected an identity crisis expressed in a disavowal of the British way of life. And so to Suez, the cold war, and on to the Falklands and Thatcher's Britain.

In his thoughtful essay mentioned earlier, Paul Greengrass has speculated about the development of the British war film after such classics as *Reach for the Sky*. He argues that the Suez crisis:

> symbolised the start of a growing tide in Britain towards iconoclastic freedom of expression on stage, screen, television and journalism. The war films of the 1960's reflect this sense of irreverence. Both *The Charge of the Light Brigade* (1968) and *King and Country* (1964), a First World War desertion drama, savaged the brutality of the military mind in ways that would have been unthinkable earlier (Greengrass, 1989, p. 36).

Such radical films, in the tradition of earlier works such as the fiercely anti-war *The Life and Death of Colonel Blimp*, directed by Michael Powell and Emeric Pressburger in 1943, have continued to be produced, as Alan Bleasdale's magnificent television drama *The Monocled Mutineer* (1987) demonstrates. A film such as *The Monocled Mutineer*, set in the First World War and addressing the issue of mutiny, is at the other end of the spectrum to *In Which We Serve*, which received the official support of the Ministry of Information. British establishment culture in the Thatcher era was especially sensitive to critical attacks on the military because, as the Falklands and the Gulf crisis demonstrate, national revival is frequently associated with strong defence and a powerful offensive capacity. Such 'preparedness' is perceived to have eventually 'won' the cold war and persuaded President Gorbachev's USSR to sue for peace and embrace capitalist values. In Thatcher's Britain, as this volume overall shows, the Falklands campaign had enormous symbolic value; to challenge it in any way was to invite the kind of official criticism levelled at Charles Wood's *Tumbledown*

(1988). The discourse of war films is thus a significant one because war touches upon some of the most fundamental apprehensions of nationhood.

Tumbledown has justly become the central dramatic text of the Falklands campaign.[5] It arose out of an article written in *The Guardian* newspaper in 1984 about Robert Lawrence, an officer in the Scots Guards who had fought in the Falklands, been seriously wounded in the battle for Tumbledown mountain before the capture of Port Stanley, and afterwards neglected by the Army bureaucracy. Charles Wood, a distinguished screenwriter and director, who had written the screenplay for such films as *The Knack* (1965), *Help!* (1965), *The Charge of the Light Brigade* and *The Long Day's Dying* (1968), became interested in Lawrence's story and contacted him. The outcome was the TV film *Tumbledown*, which attracted a vast audience: two other works associated with the production have also appeared, Charles Wood's screenplay of the film, *Tumbledown* (1987),[6] and a memoir, co-written by John Lawrence and Robert Lawrence, entitled *When the Fighting is Over: Tumbledown: A Personal Story* (1988).[7]

The background to the film's eventual appearance is interesting, as John and Robert Lawrence allege in their memoir that both the Ministry of Defence and the Scots Guards, at various stages, tried to suppress it. They suggest, for example, that slanderous stories were put out in order to discredit Robert Lawrence. The film itself received considerable publicity in the making, and, before it was televised, a scene was removed because it was considered to be factually inaccurate by a member of the Scots Guards who took part in the action. Other disputes about the film's facts centred upon the delay Robert Lawrence claimed he suffered in receiving hospital treatment; there was dispute also about the position he claimed he was placed in during the Falklands Memorial Service at St Paul's; and the Army authorities also rejected his allegations that he did not receive proper compensation from the South Atlantic Fund. *Tumbledown* received one of the largest ever audiences for a television film drama of its kind, and attracted widespread political opposition perhaps because Charles Wood had earlier been labelled as 'left wing ... subversive ... anti-establishment' (Wood, 1987, p. ix). Television and press discussion of the film was often heated and generated a considerable number of oppositional views. This controversy surrounding *Tumbledown* was also intensified by allegations by Ian Curteis that his earlier pro-Thatcher Falklands play in 1986 had been rejected by the BBC on political grounds. The film *Tumbledown* has consequently become a central ideological text.

The narrative of *Tumbledown* shifts back and forth from horrific battle scenes and related incidents of military life to the private life of Robert Lawrence who was awarded the Military Cross for gallantry in the Falklands. The central episode of the drama is the near fatal wounding and partial disablement of Lieutenant Lawrence: he was hit by a high-velocity bullet, and the back of his head blown away. He recovered from his grave injuries, although only after a long period of recuperation and rehabilitation, to walk again, to marry and to father a child. In 1989, disillusioned with Britain, and with the treatment he and other Falklands veterans received, Robert Lawrence emigrated to Australia.

The film explores Robert Lawrence's secure family life, and represents the efforts of his parents to mitigate their son's distress. Robert is born into a military family, his father a distinguished former RAF officer who is devoted to Queen and country. The young Lawrence is cushioned from the realities of a Britain suffering from urban riots and industrial decline, and enjoys many class privileges: Robert attends Fetters public school, moves on to Sandhurst, and is commissioned as an officer in the Scots Guards. The film *Tumbledown* frequently depicts him in Sloane Ranger territory, especially on the night before disembarkation to the Falklands when his actions in drinking champagne Hurrah Henry style in a Chelsea wine bar with his friend Hugh are contrasted with the pub crawl of Prothero, O'Rourke and the other guardsmen. Robert's terrain is the England of débutantes and Aston Martins, a landscape of the mind signified throughout the film and, in particular, throughout the tranquil opening shots of the Cotswolds countryside; references are later made to other English cultural icons, such as Lord's Cricket Ground. Richard Eyre's subtle direction and Charles Wood's self-refracting script[8] are suitably evasive in portraying this vanishing England, appearing both to celebrate its continuing presence and yet ironize the nostalgia it frequently attracts. The rhetoric and moral appropriateness of this version of Englishness are tested throughout *Tumbledown*.

By means of the play's visual switching and cross-cutting between country cottages and the horrors of Mount Tumbledown, the ideological poles of the drama are connected up. Robert's most significant action, when he conforms to what is expected of him by the Army, and categorically proves his manhood, is his bayoneting of the young Argentinian conscript who tries to stop him by uttering the word 'please' in broken English. This shocking scene, rendered in graphic detail and close-up, destroys forever Robert's peace of mind, separating him conclusively from formerly held naïve misconceptions of patriotic duty. Robert has always believed, like his father, in the ideals of fighting to defend Queen and country, but it is only through committing this merciless act of execution himself, and through his experiences after having been wounded that he fully *understands* what duty and patriotism can in practice demand of a soldier. Even after his suffering and the rebuffs and neglect he receives, Robert continues to believe that the Falklands campaign was a just cause: he summarizes near the end of *When The Fighting Is Over* what his experiences came to mean to him: (Lawrence and Lawrence, 1988, pp. 192–3):

When thousands of fighting troops suddenly march into your house to tell you, with the barrel of a gun stuck up your nose, that you must no longer speak English, but Spanish, you have a right to be defended by any civilized nation.

And I had, and still have, this white-hot pride. The kind of pride that the Army trains young soldiers to build up. The kind of pride that enables them to go off to war and fight and kill for what they are taught to believe in; principles like freedom of choice and of speech.

What I didn't realize, until, like so many others, I came back crippled after doing my bit for my country, was the extent to which we had been conned. Conned into believing in a set of priorities and principles that the rest of the world and British society in general no longer gave two hoots about. We had been 'their boys' fighting in the Falklands, and when the fighting was over, nobody wanted to know.

The indifference, embarrassment, exploitation and countless bureaucratic cock-ups that followed my return home were not what I'd expected. They opened my eyes. They changed me. They changed my father, a great patriot, with twenty-eight years in the RAF behind him. He believed so strongly in the forces, and believed 'the system' would look after us all. I think the reality shook him. It was almost as if a staunch Christian, who had always lived and acted in a respectful Christian way, were suddenly being made to question God.

He was always prepared to throw his weight around on my behalf, and did so after I came home. He knew the forces system, and the language of the system, and the right people he should be contacting to help me at any time. What's frightening is how much I still suffered despite having the sort of father I had, doing all that. It made me wonder, if this was happening to me, an officer with a supportive forces family, what the hell was happening to the injured Guardsman whose father was an out-of-work shipbuilder in Glasgow, or an out-of-work miner in Wales.

Ultimately, Robert retains his faith in the validity of medals, parades, military discipline and tradition, yet he comes to revile the bureaucrats and politicians who self-seekingly hide behind such custom and ceremony. Robert's continuing patriotism, as presented in the film, is, therefore, perhaps more credible than that, say, of the Vietnam veteran, Ron Kovic, in Oliver Stone's film *Born on the Fourth of July* (1989). Kovic undergoes a 'conversion' after his wounding and eventually comes 'home' to a USA that makes him 20 years later a successful media star. Robert does not undergo a conversion in Wood's play to a different set of values: he retains his principles, while realizing the high price they involve. The screenplay of *Tumbledown* is scripted in such a way that Robert is not whitewashed: he is presented throughout as a rather wild, physical, boorish and occasionally rudely outspoken young man, a plausible representation of a foolhardy soldier who is too daring for his own good. His unruly behaviour, after his terrible injury, is, of course, explicable psychologically as a post-traumatic stress condition. The photographs of his head wound, showing parts of his brain exposed, help to explain his anger, and are included in the film.

The creation of Robert Lawrence allows wider issues than the war itself to be discursively focused. British culture is shown as disowning him after the initial glory of the campaign has been absorbed: he is hidden away at the back of St Paul's Cathedral, and is treated badly by the Army authorities regarding information both about his disability pension and about compensation payments from the South Atlantic Fund. Such social rejection persuades the play's audience to question the moral worth of some of the traditions and ceremonies woven into the narrative. The Ceremony of the Keys performed at Traitor's Gate for example, is interfused with other images of national pride, such as newsreel of the Falklands Task Force returning triumphantly or of the ensuing victory parades. Although such images are powerfully communicated, they are ironically set off against other less jingoistic ones, of the wounded being brought back ignominiously to Brize Norton or of John Lawrence's handsome face, adorned by an RAF style moustache, echoing his son's words, 'It wasn't worth it'.

A similar reversal is encoded in the non-realist images superimposed on the old regimental song of the Scots Guards 'I will go, I will go'. The ironic nature of this platoon song about misplaced regimental loyalty, is suggested by the contrast between its serene musical beauty, and the pictures of crazed and bleeding soldiers giving the lie to its tonal perfection. Only if we examine the last verse, the film implies, may we fully appreciate, the true nature of warfare:

> When we came back to the glen
> Winter was turning
> Our goods lay in the snow
> And our houses were burning
> I will go, I will go.

Robert, who is a veteran of Northern Ireland, Brunei and Kenya, falls prey to the haunting rhythms of the song and its gung-ho call to duty: he fails tragically to realize the implications of its last verse. His transformation from hero to anti-hero is expressed stylistically in the manner of his wounding through Richard Eyre's impressive direction. Robert's 'Isn't this fun' posture, with two rifles blazing, cruelly parodies the celluloid bravery of John Wayne in *True Grit* (1969). Other key images reinforce this implication that *Boys' Own* heroism is increasingly obsolete in an age of mechanized war, like that of the violent shattering of the tomato hit in slow motion by a high-velocity bullet. Frequently, the discourse of images in *Tumbledown* skilfully devalues the glamour of war, as in this instance.

Tumbledown is a highly sophisticated and complex work, which dramatizes many of the profound contradictions underlying the operations of the Task Force in 1982. It is ambivalent about almost everything that took place during the conflict itself and its immediate aftermath; it endorses the courage of the troops and their professionalism, while satirizing Rambo-style heroism as fatuous. Colin Firth's portrayal of Robert refrains from taking sides and appears neither clearly pro- nor anti-war. Robert Lawrence is played as unpleasantly macho, and yet his horseplay is shown to cover up a vulnerable, sympathetic aspect of his character: his irascible, self-centred behaviour has ample motivation. Wood's screenplay also ambiguously celebrates a construction of Englishness, while deconstructing the dead weight of its tradition. The narrative contains other contradictory impulses, which are expressed through Robert's downward curve from expectant patriotism to disaffection, and his criticism of those who are unworthy custodians of his principled beliefs. The play suggests overall that the British ruling élite is lacking in a moral clarity of purpose such as that supported by Noel Coward's earlier tribute to the ideology of service, *In Which We Serve*. Unlike Coward and Lean's film, a truly united nation with a transcendent common purpose seems very far away in Thatcher's Britain. The private suffering of Robert, and his fulminations against the system, bear little resemblance to the idealized code of Captain Kinross. Robert is no Lord Mountbatten. Interestingly, the class system in *Tumbledown* is reaffirmed, as is the ideology of the English gentleman, head of the caring upper middle-class family. The drama, while representing working-class soldiers sympathetically, depicts their suffering as incidental and marginal to Robert's. The film's centre of gravity is elsewhere in exploring the hollowness of establishment values. Robert is a public schoolboy who learns through bitter experience that Thatcherism isn't always what it seems. Of course, as Alan Coren has noted, if he had *not* been wounded, he probably would have thought differently, and it almost certainly *would* have been worth it!

The mythological Falklands trip was certainly *not* worth it for Philip Williams, the protagonist of Paul Greengrass' *Resurrected*, upon whose experience the film is loosely based. In a memoir, *Summer Soldier* (1990), co-authored with Maurice Power, Williams narrates how the campaign virtually destroyed him. Like a whole series of Vietnam veterans, he suffered a complete revulsion from the ideals of the military after being medically discharged, and became caught up in drug addiction, deviant behaviour and petty criminality; he eventually served a term of imprisonment.

Summer Soldier is an angry, crude book which attacks the class bias of the Scots Guards, and also criticizes the tabloid press, which is blamed for irresponsible behaviour. Philip Williams fought in the same battle for Tumbledown Mountain as Lieutenant Robert Lawrence, although he did not actually meet him. Williams seems to have mixed feelings about *Resurrected*: while he greatly admired the acting, and observes '. . . as a film it's one of the best I've ever seen', he disassociates himself from what he perceives as its opportunism and sensationalism. He alleges that *Resurrected* was 'riding on the back of the Falklands euphoria', and also that '. . . they put in so much sensational fiction that, to my mind, they changed it from being what would have been a good historical document into just another war film . . .'.[9] Such a literal response is understandable; it does not detract from *Resurrected*'s quality as a serious imaginative study of the impact of the Falklands upon a rather uncharismatic young man and upon his working-class family living in a settled northern community.

Martin Allen's carefully crafted screenplay narrates the Lazarus-like return of a Scots Guardsman, Kevin Deakin, who goes missing for seven weeks during the assault on Port Stanley. Deakin is presumed dead, and an impressive memorial service is held for him in his native village church. The narrative explores how his parents, his girlfriend, Julie, and his local community respond to his extraordinary return, and how, after initial euphoria, Deakin is vilified as a deserter. The film concludes with scenes of army brutality, when his former comrades turn on him, hold a mock trial and punish him with a 'regimental bath'. After these injuries, he is finally discharged from the Guards.

Resurrected follows other war films in switching back and forth between Britain and the Falklands war zone: scenes that take place in his home environment or within Chelsea Barracks are explained psychologically by reference to the epiphanic moment on Tumbledown when Kevin rescued his gravely wounded friend, Johnny Fodden, and is himself disorientated by a shell burst, which causes him to lose his memory. Deakin's harrowing experiences, after returning to his Lancashire village, are primarily caused by a series of newspaper reports which build him up as a hero, and then hint that he is a deserter. Although cleared of cowardice by an enquiry, Deakin faces intolerance both from his own working class and from his snobbish commanding officer, who tells his parents 'your son was never cut out to be in a regiment of this calibre in the first place'.

The images of Britain communicated by Greengrass and Allen's film are of a harsh, inconsiderate society, over-influenced by a scandal-mongering press and underpinned by a military culture whose behaviour is little different from the violent tribalism of football hooligans. Although Deakin's parents ultimately support their son, and one of his fellow soldiers, Bonner, intercedes on his behalf, Greengrass' film is critical of the narrow working-class attitudes that have emerged in the 1980s. In place of the tolerant, older working-class values of cooperation and solidarity, *Resurrected* represents an ugly small-town mentality which finally shows little sympathy towards its own inarticulate and ungla-morous Falklands veteran. The village is shown to be easily seduced by the public myths of Falklands heroism, flattered by the attention paid to 'our' hero at his memorial service, but unable to cope with the truth that he is as unheroic as themselves. In a moment of insight, Kevin seizes on this fact: 'Just an embarrassment, aren't I, now? If I'm not a hero then I must be a deserter – well I'm neither! Bloody stupid pointless war.'

Martin Allen's script follows many generic conventions in portray-ing Kevin's ostracism. For example, his girlfriend, Julie, is unable to empathize with his changed condition and wishes for the 'old' Kevin before he left for the South Atlantic. As does *Tumbledown*, newsreel of the glorious Falklands celebrations is shown as an ironic counterpart to Kevin's confused, pacifist utterances. Kevin's familiar cultural separa-tion is recognizable also from a sequence of Vietnam war films, yet his portrayal by David Thewlis is extremely effective in its unheroic down-beat quality. As a focalizer, Kevin Deakin is totally unremarkable, a representative northern adolescent who convinces the viewer that he is rather colourless, fruit-machine-playing, Manchester City supporter. This fictive treatment of relentless ordinariness, Kevin's lack of a defence mechanism against the processes of victimization and scape-goating, is impressively communicated through Greengrass' direction. *Resurrected* situates Kevin within an alien environment of militarism, and unlike *Tumbledown*, which displays an ambiguous attitude to-wards the glorious traditions of the Scots Guards, portrays the élite guardsmen in savage terms. Their leader, Slaven, played by Ewan Stewart, is a deeply disturbed young man who has been turned into an assailant by his battle experiences. The scenes where Kevin is physically intimidated suggest that the heroic Falklands adventure has, in this instance, spawned a breed of intolerant thugs.

Whereas *Resurrected* includes the occasional violent scene, *For Queen and Country* (1989) presents social violence as an integral condi-tion of life for many British citizens, especially those of ethnic minor-ities. Martin Stellman's film descends, in neo-Darwinian fashion, to the lowest rung of the social scale to concentrate upon the struggles of what is often called the criminal underclass or, in marxist terminology, the lumpenproletariat. It is set in the urban jungle of decaying London council estates and black ghettoes, an England far removed from the country cottage culture of *Tumbledown* or the close-knit respectable working-class community of *Resurrected*. To this twilight England, excluded from the Thatcherite economic miracle of the 1980s, Reuben James, a black Falklands veteran, returns. He has joined the élite Para-chute Regiment to better himself, but having been denied promotion, leaves the army for the concrete wilderness of drug pushers and petty criminals. Mistakenly, Reuben, who has also seen active service in Northern Ireland with his close friend, Fish, believes that his military experience will be an advantage in gaining employment. He is soon disillusioned, realizing that the colour of his skin precludes him from many jobs commensurate with his abilities. Colin, a former friend and drug pusher, who has escaped from the hopelessness and despair of Reuben's vandalized high-rise flats, taunts him with the accusation that his Falklands campaign medals are now useless; in 1989 pride and honour, like service to country, have no economic currency. If he wishes to advance himself, he must exploit the capitalist system by following the rules of the marketplace. Eventually, after much provocation, Reuben temporarily joins Colin in an isolated criminal episode; the incident is monitored by the police who later use Reuben's involvement to blackmail him into becoming an informer.

The narrative of *For Queen and Country* centres on Reuben's determination to live a law-abiding life, and to obtain worthwhile and satisfying employment. Both objectives prove impossible in a society where he suffers from a twin handicap: the double stigma of being black and also of living in a 'sink' council estate. Those surrounding him confirm his negative prospects: Linford, a black former schoolfriend, is increasingly criminalized, and eventually kills a policeman by mistake; Fish, who cannot provide for his wife and children, has his electricity disconnected, and is finally killed in error. As such plot details suggest, *For Queen and Country* is a deeply pessimistic film. It is founded on the determinist law that an environment of rubbish-strewn walkways and intolerable high unemployment will inevitably breed crime, vandalism, drug-pushing and, eventually, serious civil disorder. The Britain it represents is a deeply divided one where racist police are little better than violent criminals themselves: police harassment of Blacks is endemic, and urban riots like those of 1981 are the tragic outcome. These dominant themes of racism and its associated lack of opportunity, are foregrounded in the film's concluding scenes which dramatize a Britain on the verge of civil war. Bands of looters, police with CS gas, dogs, high-velocity rifles, gangs of 'steamers' preparing for battle reinforce Linford's warning to Reuben 'This is war'. By a profound irony, the war zone has been relocated from the Falklands to Brixton and the inner cities.

For Queen and Country, which includes an exceptional performance from Denzel Washington as Reuben James, projects too much of a strident argument. Its thesis that squalor produces a polarized society with a totally disaffected underclass, alienated from all power and participation, is hammered home in menacing fashion. Stylistically, the film utilizes the eerie subworld of walkways and graffiti-marked lifts in an allegorical manner: there is a pervading oppression of spirit implied by such unlit bridges, desolate subways and stone balconies. Michael Klamer's score contributes to this hellish atmosphere. The feeling that the movie is over-didactic is supported when Reuben is deprived of his British citizenship by the delayed impact of the 1981 British Nationalities Act. Because he entered Britain from St Lucia, at the age of 4, Reuben is classed an an immigrant without rights to a British passport. He is compelled to revert to being a citizen of St Lucia, despite his military service for Queen and country. His bitter experience of rejection radicalizes Reuben and ultimately he, too, adopts the prevailing motto of the deprived British underclass, 'Ducking and diving; fucking and skiving'. He does so reluctantly and without joy. His bloody end, assassinated by a police marksman, after revenging himself on the policeman who mistakenly murdered Fish, is in keeping with the ubiquitous tone of fatality that characterizes *For Queen and Country*. It is a disturbing and angry film where the Falklands conflict is represented only as a veiled historical influence, empty of meaning: the real war is the one taking place on the streets.

British films which represent the Falklands campaign are, perhaps understandably, ethnocentric in character, taking little account of Argentine views on their Malvinas invasion. Although the three focalizers of the works we have discussed, Robert Lawrence, Kevin Deakin and Reuben James, are generally sympathetic to the poorly trained Argentine conscripts whom they fought, they were much too preoccupied with their own troubles to speculate on the wider international implications of the conflict. For an Argentine perspective, it is necessary to turn to an Argentine film, the best of which is *Veronico Cruz* (1987). Directed by Miguel Pereira, *Veronico Cruz*, which narrates the life and death of its eponymous hero, is a poetic, lyrical study of Argentine country people who live in a remote, beautiful mountainous region. The Argentina it represents is essentially an older, traditional indigenous culture, hardly affected by urbanization or modern lifestyles. Above all, this is how the adolescent boy *sees* his environment.

Veronico symbolizes the innocence of such a vanishing society: his mother dies, and his father abandons him, which leaves him particularly receptive to outside influences. When his grandmother also dies, he is adopted by a caring and gentlemanly schoolteacher. The schoolteacher acts as the lens through which we follow Veronico's story. He takes the boy in search of his father, a political prisoner of the junta. Eventually, Veronico is killed when the *General Belgrano* is sunk by the British submarine. *HMS Conqueror.*

At work in the film are two contradictory forces, the pull towards a tranquil existence in the idyllic mountain regions and its opposite, the negative and inevitable impact of the fascist 1980s. The peaceful Jujuy Province with its pastoral villages cannot remain immune from the corrupt political actions of the junta. Throughout the film, there are many hints of the tragic outcome of 1982; for example, the boy experiences a premonition of war when he has a nightmare vision of sheep in their fold killed by a savage lion-like beast. This is followed later by surreal shots of the head of a sheep on a pole. Later still, another sequence similarly adumbrates the forthcoming slaughter of the innocents, when there are disturbing images of blood from dead cattle spattered on a cowshed's walls. Veronico himself is shown as contributing unwittingly to his own death; for he is an avid reader of books and comics describing maritime life and naval adventure. He dreams of being a naval hero in a mythical world of pirates and sailing ships.

The teacher tries to educate him into reality by warning him that the sea is an environment where people must work hard in order to make a living, but the boy is unwilling to forgo his romantic dreams. One of the many effective scenes that warn us of impending tragedy in true Latin American 'style of destiny' is an occasion when the boy plays on the parched river flats; this registers symbolically the true sterility of the raped land. An armed vehicle appears, which Veronico fatefully touches. The sensitive flute-playing boy, who admires sea-shells, represents the spirit of Argentina's youth, later needlessly lost in the futile confrontation with Britain.

During the course of the film, the boy, accompanied by the teacher, visits monuments marking the founding of the nation, and is impressed by the statue of General Belgrano, the true father of Argentina. Veronico also sits on the throne of labour, unconsciously expressing his affinity with the working people of his country. Meanwhile the teacher is temporarily arrested, interrogated, and the frightening reality of the 'disappeared' and the tortured intrudes into the boy's fantasy world. Shots of the steelworks, and of the Argentine flag, ironically made in Hong Kong, a British colony, ground the film in the situation of impending war. On one level, the narrative may be read in this way, foregrounding its historical topicality; on another, it signifies a subtle desconstruction of the Latinist myth of masculinity, threaded around the search for a responsible and good father. Clearly, the 'fatherless' boy yearns for this true father, the imprisoned Castilo Cruz, and luckily finds a surrogate in his compassionate teacher. Ultimately, though, by being killed in battle Veronico himself leaves a fatherless child; for his girlfriend was pregnant when he left for war. In the nation's affairs the legitimate, historical father, General Belgrano, is supplanted by the degenerate Galtieri. The recurrent theme of absent fathers is an interesting one: in their symbolic absence, the children of the village make do with heroizing footballers, such as Ardiles, Kempes and Passarella. *Veronico Cruz* thus counteracts the myth of *machismo* in its two central characters, the sensitive schoolboy and the reflective teacher, who allows full rein to the gentler, more feminine side of his character. The teacher resembles an English gentleman of the Noel Coward era.

The gentle lyricism of *Veronico Cruz* contrasts with another hispanic version of the psychological impact of 1982, Jorge Blanco's surreal black comedy film *Argie* (1985), which narrates the absurdist experiences of an Argentine man living in London at the height of the Falklands War, who decides to fight back unilaterally against the British. The narrative subverts realism through the totally implausible, fatuous actions of the central character who attempts rape, fires arrows at a jingoistic neighbour, picks a fight in a pub and becomes involved in a bizarre, non-realist execution by firing squad. *Argie* is unsuccessful in its attempt to satirize British jingoism, and lapses into totally disconnected incident without a political or ideological polemic emerging as a rhetoric of persuasion. Its gestures towards post-modernist parody and superimposition sadly do not work because it has neither an argument nor a radical point of view which is dramatized effectively. More orthodox sources are probably better in evaluating the Argentine experiences of their South Atlantic defeat, such as Martin Middlebrook's (1989) excellent book, *The Fight For The Malvinas: The Argentine Forces in the Falklands War.*[10]

As source material for studying the Falklands conflict, films offer notoriously unreliable historical evidence: like other forms of popular cultural expression, their images of war are partial and selective. Nevertheless, the three films portraying the British side of the campaign, and, indeed, the Argentine movie, *Veronico Cruz*, are all challenging artefacts. Their narratives fulfil the criteria of serious, imaginative works of art: they are critical, enquiring and their metaphors provoke public controversy.[11] In style, *Tumbledown*, *Resurrected* and *For Queen and Country* are harsher, more abrasive than the romantic, pastoral Argentine film, which may be owing to the fact that the former are concerned with how veterans angrily confront an intolerant society which does not value their war service. It is interesting that two of the British films, *Tumbledown*, and *Resurrected*, are associated with television, which assisted with their funding and production facilities. David Puttnam is reported as saying recently that his blockbuster, *Memphis Belle* (1990), ought really to have been about the crew of a Lancaster bomber, but the demands of an insular US audience prevented such a story. When *In Which We Serve* was made, the British film industry was powerful enough to make commercially successful films, a situation which has long since vanished. It is therefore greatly to the credit of Paul Greengrass, Martin Allen, Charles Wood and Richard Eyre, and to BBC Television and Channel 4, that such radical war films can still be made in the UK. *Tumbledown*, in particular, through its experimental use of flashbacks and cutting, is a technically sophisticated work that is likely to become a classic war film. Its complex and ambivalent attitudes to patriotism, duty and the values associated with the English gentleman give it an edge over the other two films treating the suffering of Falklands veterans. Ironically, the Argentine film, *Veronica Cruz*, throughout its lyrical narrative, counters impending doom by means of a character, the schoolteacher, who displays many of the virtues traditionally associated with the English gentleman. Art recognizes no frontiers!

British war films treating the Falklands depict a country very different from the unified motherland represented in Coward and Lean's *In*

Which We Serve; in place of the earlier images of a common national purpose, Thatcher's England has seemingly generated its antithesis, a divided culture and a polarized society. Despite public proclamations and government rhetoric about a restoration of national pride, the Dunkirk spirit is conspicuously missing in such films as *Tumbledown* and *Resurrected. For Queen and Country* goes even further in portraying a totally disunited kingdom unworthy of the dutiful service of its Falklands veterans.

Notes

1 Dalyell, T. (1982). *One Man's Falklands*. London, Cecil Woolf, p. 129.
2 *The Late Show* (1990). BBC Television, 4 September.
3 Fountain, N. (1990). 'The human cost of bloodthirsty bombast', *The Guardian*, 29 August, p. 32.
4 Greengrass, P. (1989). 'The Falklands myth begins to crumble', *Sunday Correspondent*, 4 September, p. 36.
5 *Tumbledown* (1988). Directed by Richard Eyre and written by Charles Wood; was shown on BBC 1 on 31 May.
6 Wood, C. (1987). *Tumbledown: A Screenplay*. Harmondsworth, Penguin.
7 Lawrence, J. and Lawrence, R. (1988). *When The Fighting is Over: A Personal Story of the Battle for Tumbledown Mountain and its Aftermath*. London, Bloomsbury.
8 Coren, A. (1988). 'Review of *Tumbledown*', *The Mail on Sunday*, 5 June, p. 37.
9 Williams, P., with Power, M. (1990). *Summer Soldier: The True Story of the Missing Falklands Guardsman*. London, Bloomsbury, p. 206.
10 Middlebrook, M. (1989). *The Fight for the Malvinas: The Argentine Forces in the Falklands War*. London, Viking.
11 See, for example, Usher, P. (1988). 'BBC play on Falklands "will shock"', *Daily Star*, 31 October.

| **3** | Whose War is it Anyway? The Argentine Press during the South Atlantic Conflict

Nick Caistor

In 1982, Argentine journalism was in a mess along with the rest of the country. Ever since 1966, a variety of regimes had restricted press freedom, often brutally. This repression reached a new ferocity under the military junta which seized power from the Peronist Government in a coup on 24 March 1976. According to the Argentine National Commission on Disappeared People, who published the report *Nunca Mas*,[1] about 100 Argentine journalists disappeared after the coup, meeting the same fate as almost 9000 of their compatriots.

All news of this campaign by the military against fellow Argentines whom they saw as 'subversive' was forbidden in the national press. Instead, a set of guidelines was established by the junta, which included the following Principles to be followed:

1 Foster the restitution of fundamental values which contribute to the integrity of society, such as: order–labour–hierarchy–responsibility–identity–honesty, etc. within the context of Christian morals.
2 Preserve the defence of the family institution.
3 Tend towards the informative and formative elements which contribute towards the Nation's cultural enrichment in its widest spectrum.
4 Offer and promote, for youth, social models which answer to the values mentioned above, to replace and eradicate the present ones.
5 Strictly respect people's dignity, private life, honour, fame and reputation.[2]

In the face of this combination of terror and ideological manipulation, the Argentine mainstream press kept quiet about the horrors. One local English-language newspaper which did report disappearances, *The Buenos Aires Herald*, found that its editors were repeatedly threatened, and forced to leave the country. The proprietor of the newest national daily published in Buenos Aires, Jacobo Timerman of *La Opinión*, was secretly captured, tortured and held in a clandestine jail for over a year before being allowed abroad to Israel.[3]

The other national dailies and weekly illustrated magazines were mainly sympathetic to the military government anyway. Some like *La Prensa* were anti-Peronist; others like *La Nación* agreed with the junta's economic policies of bringing Argentina more into the international economy, ending protectionism and encouraging agricultural exports as against encouraging local industry. They published as news the communiqués issued by the military junta, and elaborated on this 'news' with versions provided for them by the military 'intervenor' assigned to each publication to make sure they had understood the message correctly.

But by the start of 1982, military rule was faltering. They no longer had the excuse of fighting 'subversives'; their economic plans were failing, and despite the compliant press, they had been unable to keep the Argentines in sympathy with their efforts. The only way that the military could unite the nation behind them was to find a spectacular course of action which no one would disagree with. When General Leopoldo Galtieri unceremoniously tipped his predecessor General Roberto Viola from power in December 1981, he was already planning an invasion of the Falklands/*Malvinas* as the surest and easiest way of bringing this about. This was a just cause shared by all Argentines, who were taught at school that the *Malvinas son Argentinas*, that the British had invaded them in 1833 and refused since then all arguments based on legality, common sense, or the force of destiny aimed at persuading them to return the islands to their rightful owners. General Galtieri and the other armed forces' chiefs knew that if they retook the Malvinas they would not have to 'convince' the press to go along with them, but could count on their enthusiastic support, while the old methods of persuasion were still in place just in case.

A good example of this was the national daily *La Prensa*, founded as early as 1869. The newspaper had been shut down by the first Peronist Government from 1951 to 1956, and was strongly against the Peronists again in the early 1970s, supporting the military government both in its fight against 'subversives' and in its economic programme. But by 1981, *La Prensa* had become disillusioned with the way things were going. One columnist, Manfred Schonfeld, began criticizing the extravagant projects the military government was spending foreign loans on, few of which ever seemed to get finished. Schonfeld was set on and badly beaten up as a warning in June 1981. Another *La Prensa* columnist, José Iglesias Rouco, was charged in July 1981 with 'endangering national peace and security' after he published secret documents relating to another affair which had nearly brought Argentina to war: the dispute with Chile over boundaries in the Beagle Channel in the far south. As a consequence, the military junta withdrew official advertising

– an important source of income for all Argentine publications – from *La Prensa*.[4]

Yet even before the Argentine takeover of the Malvinas on 2 April, the same José Iglesias Rouco was urging that everyone back the armed forces' initiative. His article in the 30 March issue of the newspaper attacked the trade unionists who had called a protest march against social conditions in Argentina for 1 April in the following terms:

> ... at stake [in the recuperation of the *Malvinas*] are principles of national sovereignty which are precisely those frequently invoked – rather too readily – by trade union leaders when it is a question of attacking the government for what they call their economic policies of 'surrender' of our national heritage – including in this the state concerns that are being 'privatised' – to foreign powers or multinationals.

From this and other laudatory articles, it seemed as though the Argentine military had immediately succeeded in their first objective: the battle to win over their own people. Whereas they had found it extremely difficult to persuade everyone that their campaign against their political opponents whom they called 'subversives' was being carried out in the name of the nation, they were now the true guardians of 'our national dignity', as Rouco put it the next day, 1 April 1982. He went on to praise the Armed Forces in glowing terms, specifically contrasting what they were now embarked upon with their earlier actions, although of course neither his newspaper nor any of the others had reported or commented on these at the time:

> ... this will be remembered as the military regime's major triumph, together with its triumph over subversion; with the difference that the methods employed and the political and moral cost of this action as compared to the so-called 'dirty war' do not compromise the spirit, the public life, or the conscience of the Argentines. Quite the opposite: they magnify them.

This immediate acceptance and glorification of the military's definition of the national good was reflected throughout the Argentine press.[5] Nearly all the politicians consulted agreed – as did the trade unionists who had been protesting only days earlier. Almost the only voice against the takeover of the islands was that of the man who became president a year later, Raúl Alfonsín, but he was denied any platform for his views.

Clarín, a mass-circulation 'serious tabloid' which published the politicians' opinions, had the front-page headline on 3 April of: 'POPULAR EUPHORIA AT THE RECUPERATION OF THE *MALVINAS*' over a photograph showing General Galtieri greeting the crowds in the Plaza de Mayo square from the balcony of the presidential palace in Buenos Aires. This was the balcony from which General Peron traditionally

Fig. 5   Sabát, *Carlos Gardel, Juan Domingo Perón y Leopoldo Fortunato Galtieri, Clarin,* 4 April 1982.

harangued his faithful, filling the square beneath; prior to this, no one in the military juntas since 1976 had been willing to challenge this memory. Now Galtieri was deliberately assuming Perón's mantle, even though the Armed Forces had overthrown a Peronist Government. A cartoon in *Clarín* the next day by Sabát made this identification explicit (Fig. 5). Sabat drew General Galtieri and Perón arm-in-arm congratulating each other. The third figure joining in the congratulations is the legendary tango singer Carlos Gardel. Although Gardel died in an aircrash in 1936, he was still a national hero in the 1980s, and he reappears in Sabat's cartoons throughout the South Atlantic conflict as the image of the best of Argentina: the pure, sentimental common man who can rise to greatness. That he should be shown congratulating Galtieri was perhaps even more of a shock than to have Galtieri equated with Perón (see Chapter 5 for further discussion of cartoon).

The two main mass-circulation colour magazines, *Siete Días* and *Gente*, were even more fervently patriotic. Throughout the weeks of the conflict, they were filled with pages of photographs, human interest reports and enthusiastic editorial comment. Yet *Gente* discussed the whole nature of *patria* ('home country') in its 22 April 1982 issue in sombre terms. In an 'Open Letter to a Soldier in the South', there is an admission that the young Argentine soldiers who are pictured on the front cover:

> ... don't have a great example of what a home country (*patria*) can be. They must have a blurred, confused image of what it means.

We have not succeeded in showing them the proper way, irrefutable truths, conduct worthy of emulation. They have not even been able to choose their way of life, to use a vote to get rid of so many failures and frustrations.

It may well be that behind their faces in the photographs they are fed up with all the grandiloquent words, with the way that all our most sacred national values have been bandied about. They probably reject all the lies, dishonesty, unkept promises, democracies which betray their true essence, all the political deals, wonder what happened to all the ideals that were never achieved.

No, they cannot have many worthy images in their adolescent minds, images that would compel them to defend something so important as the home country, or risk losing something so irreplaceable as their lives.

The piece ends on the more optimistic note that these adolescents will show the rest of Argentina 'a better country': the youth of Argentina has by its sacrifice been won back from the temptation of 'subversion' and has now found its true dimensions. This idea that the retaking of the *Malvinas* was an ordeal by fire thanks to which the nation would emerge purified was a theme common to much of the Argentine press.

Alongside this article, *Gente* published a logo in which Falklands Islands 1833 had been crossed out, and substituted by 1982 *ISLAS MALVINAS*. This renaming with the 'proper' Spanish term was a constant preoccupation of Argentine magazines and newspapers throughout the conflict; the two versions immediately dramatize the vying claims for ownership of the islands. Maps of the islands featured constantly, with the largely invented Spanish names on them. Sometimes it took the publications a while to catch up: *La Prensa* at first had its reporter in Puerto Stanley, but this very quickly became *Puerto Argentino*. News from London of the battle of Goose Green was given in *Clarín*: the next day the place had become *Prado de los Gansos* (a literal translation from the English).

This naming in Spanish was seen as an essential part of the struggle for Argentine sovereignty. It was symbolic of Argentina's emergence as a power with the right to raise its flag on territory and claim it as its own. But perhaps the Argentine press difficulties in naming places on the islands reflected a hesitation born of the fact that the British had been on the islands for 150 years and so named things through use rather than from abstract principle. Bestowing a name confers and confirms legitimacy; but behind the bombast, the Argentines were perhaps unsure of their claims: even the ill-fated *General Belgrano* started life as a Second World War US battle-cruiser, before being bought and renamed by the Argentines in 1951.

This uncertainty was also apparent in the Argentine press reasoning behind why Argentina was at war with Britain. In the twentieth century, Argentina has often regarded itself as an emerging world power. Early in the century, it saw itself as a serious rival to the USA, since the new waves of immigrants arriving in its cities would lead it to still greater prosperity in what was then the stablest of Latin American democracies.[6] Although this hope of progress was not fulfilled, the Argentines still considered they dealt with the USA and European countries on an equal footing. The military junta which took power in 1976 saw Argentina as a vital part of what was often called 'Western Christian civilization', and most Argentines shared this opinion. Any talk of Argentina as a dependent quasi-colony in the global capitalist economy, or of the North–South divide, was rejected as being terminology only used by the marxist subversives who were attempting to destroy the very soul of Argentina.

Yet the 'recuperation' of the *Malvinas* was immediately interpreted in precisely this way. The 2 April editorial in *Clarín* expressed the hope that 'we can therefore legitimately expect the government in London to accept that the historic era in which it could take possession of territorial fragments which do not belong to it is now well and truly over'. *La Prensa*, on the same day, was even more explicit:

> Colonialism is dead, and Great Britain has accepted the fact, except in the case of Argentina's southern Atlantic islands. This is inexplicable, because there is no way of denying the will of our people to recuperate the islands nor, as the briefest of analyses of the situation shows, is there any way Great Britain can go against the nature of things and the progress of the destiny of humanity.

Columnists in magazines such as *El Porteño* wrote in the May 1982 edition that this was 'THE NORTH AGAINST THE SOUTH', placing Argentina firmly in with those countries united by their common suffering from 'hunger and unemployment, inflation and dictatorships, monoculture and piecework'. A writer in the 5 May 1982 issue of *La Prensa* roundly announced: 'the battle for the *Malvinas* constitutes the first armed confrontation in the new strategic era ... which divides the north and south of our modern world'. This new kind of thinking led to the strangest alliances: another Sabát cartoon in *Clarín* on 7 June 1982 showed Carlos Gardel once more, this time shaking hands with Fidel Castro, the president of revolutionary Cuba and head of the non-aligned movement. In the previous six years, any such cartoon would have been anathema to the military authorities.

Although the Argentine press analysed the war in these terms, and were all sure that their country's cause was just, they had little experience of actually reporting a war. In this century, Argentina had not been to war before (it joined the Second World War on the side of the allies the day before the armistice) with the result that the press did not have much idea of how to picture the enemy. The only war the military government in power in 1982 had fought was against fellow Argentines, which the press had largely silenced. The Argentine press had no quarrel with Britain – for many years, it had been portrayed as a powerful model for the Argentines. British journalists and others in Argentina during the time of the war agreed how little personal animosity there was towards them, as the Argentines insisted that there was no hatred of the British, simply a determination to 'recuperate' something that belonged to them.

The result of this was that the Argentine press reached back into history for their portrayal of the British; the most common view was that of the British as pirates. The May issue of *El Porteño* showed Mrs Thatcher with eye-patch, skull and crossbones on her hat, wielding a cutlass. The publisher's letter inside continued the theme:

> We know what is at stake and who our opponents are – we should not confuse the great Shakespeare with the treacherous Captain Morgan, who betrayed his own kind when he invaded Panama, thus breaking the strict pirate code of honour, stealing the Spanish gold taken by fellow pirates from the Spanish crown, which was then used to bring wealth to the British Isles. Surprisingly, this same spirit still exists in Britain, denying all rights to any country it disdains, not just Argentina.

Magazines like *Gente* took this a step further. They insisted throughout that the Argentines would be the 'gentlemen', whereas the English would cheat and act in an underhand, piratical way. The Argentines did retake the *Malvinas* without killing anyone – the only casualty was one of their own men, Captain Giachino. *Gente* made much of this, not only entitling their report: 'WHILE THE ARGENTINES FOUGHT WITHOUT KILLING, THE ENGLISH SHOT HIM IN THE BACK', but giving a lurid account of his death:

> 'Cover me', Giachino told his men. Then with a grenade in each hand, he ran to the centre of the yard, calling on the English marines to surrender 'or I'll throw these grenades' . . .

This was at the start of the war. As events unfolded, the news generated from the Argentine side became limited to official communiqués. The newspapers had no correspondents of their own with the Argentine forces on the islands, and so had no first-hand reports apart from the ones sent through the official news agency, Telam. The magazines and newspapers relied on what they could get via the wires from London and elsewhere.

This dearth extended to photographs and 'colour' items, so that Argentine readers more often saw Mrs Thatcher, John Nott and the British war cabinet rushing about than they did their own rulers. There were reports of arguments in the Commons, a peace march in London, and for example on 11 June 1982 nearly all the Argentine newspapers included a photo of someone in London reading the *Evening Standard* with the banner headline 'The Pain and the Courage', duly translated into Spanish in the caption. These photographs were not included to play up how demoralized the enemy was; although all the Argentine press also carried pictures of British ships in flames – Martin Cleaver's famous picture of *HMS Antelope* for example – they were not used to glorify Argentine action (*HMS Antelope* was relegated to the inside pages) as much as because they were the only images available. The effect of this was to give the impression that it was only the British who were fighting the war, so that beyond the initial euphoria, the Argentines were once again robbed of the sense that this was something they were participating in directly for themselves.

In part, this could be seen as confirmation that the South Atlantic war was indeed a conflict between the technologized North and the underdeveloped South, so that the Argentine media found itself swamped with readily available material supplied from Britain and the USA rather than generated in Argentina. In part also though, this silence was due to the suspicions and fears of the Argentine Armed Forces, who were not sure they could count on controlling the reactions of their own public. Just as all news of the earlier 'war' against the 'subversives' in Argentina had been suppressed, so they now would not permit any free flow of news generated on the *Malvinas* or in Buenos Aires. The most eloquent example of this perhaps concerned the text of the final surrender of Argentine troops in Port Stanley. On 17 June 1982, *La Prensa* carried a copy of this in a wire photo from London. At the bottom of the Spanish translation, there was a Note From the Editor: 'No information about this document was available from Buenos Aires.'

Notes

1 Argentina's Commission on Disappeared People (1986). *Nunca Más*. London, Faber and Faber, pp. 362–4.
2 Simpson, J. and Bennett, J. (1985). *The Disappeared: Voices from a Secret War*. London, Robson Books, p. 234.
3 Graham-Yooll, A. (1984). *The Press in Argentina from 1973–1980*. London, Writers and Scholars Trust, pp. 117–118.
4 Ibid., pp. 179–180.
5 For a discussion of the Argentine media during the South Atlantic War, see 'The regimented society', in Burns, J. (1987). *The Land that Lost its Heroes: The Falklands, the Post-War and Alfonsín*. London, Bloomsbury, pp. 68–85.
6 Cf. *Argentina Between the Great Powers, 1939–1946*. London, Macmillan, 1989, pp. 34–35.

cipal members, Leonard Rosoman, who had been an official war artist himself during the Second World War. At the time of the decision to send the Task Force, there had been an exhibition of Kitson's work on display at the Workshop Gallery, London, with drawings detailing the operations of *The Times* newspaper offices. Rosoman recalls simply asking Kitson at the private view if she was interested in going, to which Kitson replied, 'When would you like me to go?'[4] It seems, however that this casual, anecdotal account leaves out the most plausible explanation for her selection – that Kitson was of the officer class by birth and also at 37 of the same age group. She had good credentials in that her grandfather was a retired naval captain and her cousin, Sir Frank Kitson, held the rank of Lieutenant-Colonel. This did not make it any easier to get her on board because of a longstanding Navy ban on women sailing on either warships themselves or on ships requisitioned on a war footing. It seems reasonable to suppose that had anyone actually placed a higher probability on the possibility of hostilities that Kitson would not have been allowed on board. According to Angela Weight, Keeper of Art at the Imperial War Museum and a member of the Artistic Records Committee, an artist would not have been commissioned in the sure knowledge that they would be entering a combat zone.[5] As it was, she was supposed to have disembarked from the *QE2* at Ascension Island. These points are pertinent when we come to consider the disparity between what the Imperial War Museum originally expected Kitson to produce and the public expectation that she would be able to display some form of unique, almost magical insight into the grim reality of combat which they had been denied in the press through censorship.

When Kitson was landed on the Falklands on 2 June 1982, she was moved about behind the lines by helicopter – staying on until 17 July 1982 to record the immediate aftermath of the war. Using black conté crayon and a variety of sketchbook sizes, her drawings are quick and animated, lines tending to describe whole forms with single quavering strokes. Partly, this is a stylistic device (as is clearly evident from the drawings she produced while on board the *QE2* while still in temperate or warm climates), partly the result of working in extreme cold, wind and rain which prevented drawing for more than 20 minutes at a stretch.

Where the action has passed life is curiously uneventful and routine. There is much waiting around or moving about of equipment and supplies (Fig. 6). Kitson's drawings are in the tradition of the war artist as reporter exemplified in the Second World War by artists such as Anthony Gross and Feliks Topolski. She has said of her interest in representing different forms of structured life outside the public domain that, 'Unlike journalists and photographers, my interest is not in the moments of news and crisis, but in how people live alongside it.'[6] Occasionally, this direction of interest, necessarily constrained on the

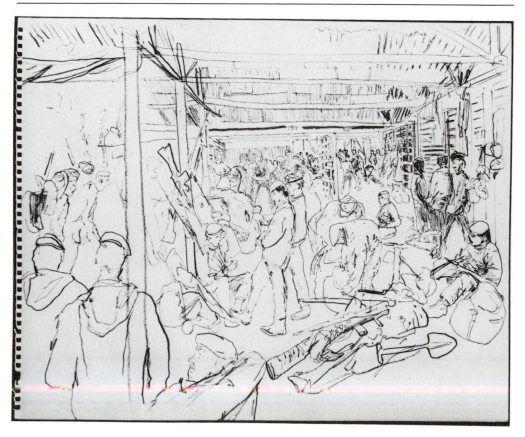

Fig. 6 Linda Kitson, *Sheepsheds at Fitzroy – 2nd Battalion Scots Guards* (1982). (By kind permission of the Trustees of the Imperial War Museum.)

Falklands themselves, allows her to pick up revealing contradictions, as on the voyage south where the Signals Squadron are seen laying out maps in the Rudolf Steiner Hairdressing Salon of the *SS Canberra* (Fig. 7). The drawing is humorous because it brings together incompatible extremes of socially structured male and female domains. The attributes of 'femininity' described by Kitson – 'Pink hairdryers, floral decorations, mauve seats, basins and model hairdo photographs'[7] – are embodied in the fixtures of the room and in its function. These are contrasted with the male concern directed away from immediate surroundings towards an altogether different terrain – one of battle plans and the recapture of sovereign territory. The female is present only as an absence indicated by attributes which imply a frivolous world concerned wholly with physical attractiveness, while the male is not only physically present but actively engaged in an exercise of knowledge and power. These constructions were played out constantly in the press where nineteenth-century notions that 'women weep while men go to war'

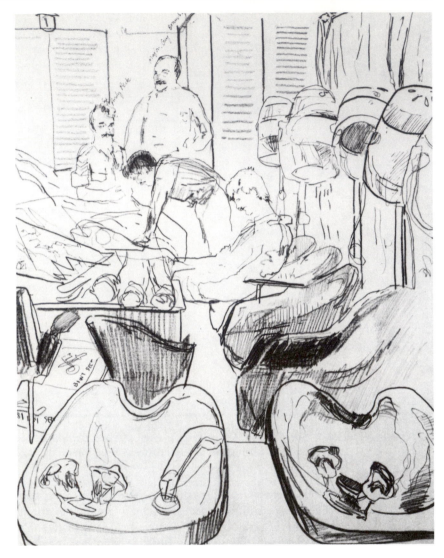

Fig. 7   Linda Kitson, *The Rudolf Steiner Hairdressing Salon, SS Canberra*
(1982). (By kind permission of the Trustees of the Imperial War Museum.)

were re-invented and held firmly in place. What Kitson does, knowingly
or otherwise, is to find and describe such an operation of patriarchal
control within the daily life of the Task Force.

An examination of the media reception of Linda Kitson's work when
it was displayed on her return is instructive as it reveals the extent to
which neither she nor her artistic production were assimilable within
the stereotypes available for either women or artistic images of war. She
produced a preliminary selection of sketches before the press on

3 August 1982 and a larger display opened at the Imperial War Museum on 4 November 1982. Press interest focused primarily on her physical appearance – 'This 37-year-old punk-haired pacifist in green and black striped drainpipes'[8] – on the physical conditions under which she worked[9] and on the fact that an avowed pacifist was paying tribute to the British troops.[10] The press was evidently unimpressed by Kitson's work, though picking up on her own description of her drawings as 'squiggles'.[11] A 'running record' of the war (as Kitson described it) which avoided both evident acts of heroism or images of blood and guts was considered to be 'drastically uninformative in terms both of emotional mood and technical content'.[12] Expecting either condemnation or sensationalism, the engagement with the everyday life of the Task Force which Kitson's drawings reveal was largely left out of discussion in the press.

While Kitson's work necessarily demonstrates an emotive response to a community (the military) in which circumstances dictated that she become an active member and not just an observer, other artists away from the war have produced work dealing with the Falklands in relation to wider issues of cultural and ideological debate that have developed within British art in the 1980s.

During this period there has been a perceived crisis in the visual arts leading to the breakdown of modernist practice under increasing commodification. It has been replaced by a pluralism in which on the one hand artists have pursued a method, associated with post-modernism, which seeks to demonstrate that art's claims to 'expression' are relative, partial and contingent through an emphasis on surface and self-referentiality, and on the other they have attempted to place art back within the social body through various forms of 'critical' realism.[13] Artists dealing with the Falklands as both a historical and a symbolic event have largely been associated with this latter tendency and their work has often been disseminated within a cultural context of thematic exhibitions in regional and national galleries and institutions partially or wholly funded by the state. It is perhaps indicative of the decline of art's power to startle and provoke within the increasingly penetrative commodifying system of late capitalism that this can be so. Nevertheless, despite the inevitable failure of political affect, there has been a substantial amount of work produced since 1982 which exposes the workings of Thatcherite ideology and its use of the Falklands War as its hour of apotheosis.

One strategy adopted by 'critical realist' artists has been to employ social satire which involves an incorporation of the techniques of cartoon and caricature within the ambit of fine art production. Jock McFadyen's work is fairly representative of this current. His work deals with the effects of social change in Margaret Thatcher's Britain using a panoply of physiological types inspired by George Grosz and in this respect his work is a conscious echo of the socially committed work of the Artists International Association in the 1930s. In *With Singing*

Fig. 8 Jock McFadyen, *With Singing Hearts ... Throaty Roarings* (1983). (By kind permission of the Trustees of the Imperial War Museum.)

Hearts ... Throaty Roarings (1983) (Fig. 8), McFadyen shows the dockside scenes on the return of the Task Force with an ugly assemblage of bull-necked nationalists swelling the foreground. As an indictment of the media celebration of victory as if it were any other form of public spectacle its message is forceful, yet McFadyen, by focusing his attentions on the failure of individuals fails to penetrate the deeper workings of the ideological system which creates such spectacular events. In this respect, artists using more dialectical methods have been more successful in identifying the operations of ideology in the legitimation of the war.

The interventionist methods adopted by feminist art practice in the 1980s came in large part through the theorization of photography and the use of structuralist and post-structuralist methodologies to identify and expose the workings of male-dominated rhetoric. Within this context, it had become possible for an artist like the Leeds-based Rosalind Furniss to apply the critically discursive possibilities of mixing collage and photographically derived images to an exploration of more deeply seated social formations in relation to certain images produced by the war. In her collages, such as *It's a Full Life in the Army* (1982) (Fig. 9), she picks up on themes related to those wryly uncovered in some of Kitson's drawings. Here, a photograph of the Paratroopers pounding the decks of the *Canberra* taken by Max Hastings (then of *The London Standard*), is reworked and juxtaposed with the display card from a boys' war toy, where the element of pre-adolescent role-playing fantasy is further indicated by comic book explosions and typical graphic sound effects. Furniss focuses particularly on the highly charged symbol of the Union Jack, which in the photographic source literally serves to mask the seat of phallic power (Hastings' photograph showed the Paras wearing Union Jack shorts). The use of hand-applied text, concomitant with theoretical understanding of the image as 'text', further serves to comment on how, in a patriarchal system, war and its preparations are embedded and disguised in the apparently innocent game of soldiers, or in the subtle conflation of physical fitness, male narcissism and military capacity. The inscriptions are quotations from body-building adverts which appeal to male vanity by proposing 'the fabulous Power-Release programme' as the way to get 'back into shape and fighting fit', while the toy shop-display card carries the imaginary trade-name, 'Playtime'. From boyhood to manhood society legitimates violence through its naturalization within the realm of male leisure interests.

A re-evaluation of the dialectical power of photomontage, or collage with photographically derived images, proved to be a significant strategy for socially engaged art in early 1980s Britain. Drawing on the tradition of politically directed photomontage exemplified by John Heartfield's work in Weimar and Nazi Germany, artists like Peter Kennard, Michael Peel and David Evans have used the medium to draw out the contradictions inherent in the rhetoric of the dominant ideology of Margaret Thatcher's Britain. The photomontage gains its effect in reproduction and not in its existence as a unique cultural object. In this respect, it can enter the social body through its dissemination in various aspects of the graphic arts: posters, postcards, LP covers, magazines, etc.

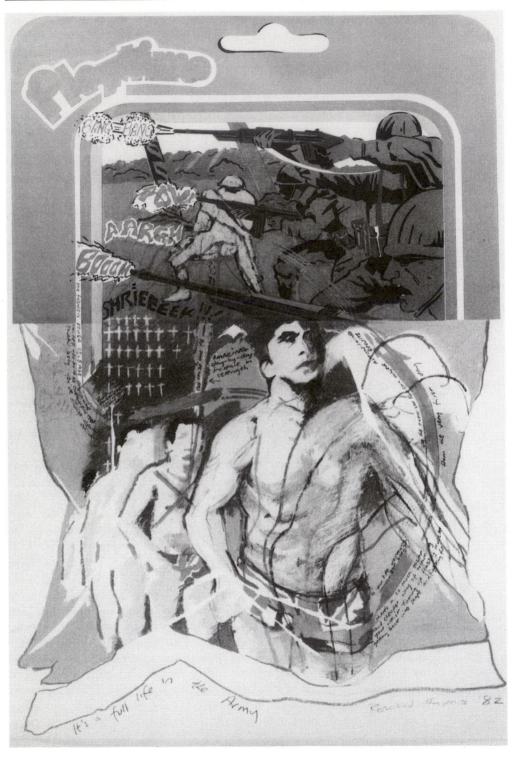

Fig. 9   Rosalind Furniss, *It's a Full Life in the Army* (1982). (By kind permission of the artist.)

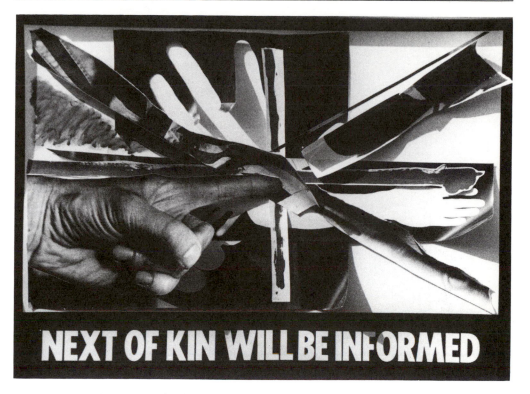

Fig. 10   Michael Peel, *Rejoice, Rejoice II* (detail) (1982). (By kind permission of the artist.)

Aware of the disguised but heavily symbolic function of the documentary photograph, Kennard, Peel and Evans combine these with photographs staged in the studio to question the analogical truth value of such images. In popular currency, the objective authority of the photograph resides in its demonstrable correspondence to something, someone or some event. It whispers 'I was there' and by identification places the viewer in proximity to what it purports to show. What Roland Barthes demonstrated was how this truth claim is in fact mediated, anchored or distorted by its textual context. The photograph, especially when used in the press, appears to support the text but, 'it is not the image which comes to elucidate or "realize" the text, but the latter which comes to sublimate, patheticize or rationalize the image'.[14]

In Michael Peel's triptych, *Rejoice, Rejoice II* (1982) (Fig. 10), the artist collaged together photographs of limbs and communications cables and built them into the form of the Union Jack which he then crudely coloured in slashes of red and blue paint. The authority invested in the flag as the symbol for which the soldier should lay down his life is contemptuously questioned. Underneath each of the three panels of the vertically arranged work, the phrase 'Next of Kin Will be Informed'

Fig. 11   Peter Kennard, *Falklands Medal* (1983). (By kind permission of the artist.)

is repeated in the matter-of-fact and deadpan language of official bureaucracy in a way which recalls the strange detachment of Ian McDonald's delivery during his press briefings. Peter Kennard's critical photomontage (Fig. 11)[15] uses, with characteristic directness and acuity, one of the two key iconic images of the war, Martin Cleaver's photograph of the exploding *HMS Antelope*; the other being the anonymous photograph of the sinking *Belgrano*. The seductive aestheticized qualities of Cleaver's image of the silhouetted ship surrounded by a pluming halo of flame had immediately attracted the attentions of newspaper picture editors aware that it could be used to fit in with a glamorizing narrative of the conflict and with the time-worn, Robert Capa-inspired search for the moment of death. The image has since been continuously recycled in magazines and books on the war and was an obvious focus of attention for artists whose experience of the conflict was its media presentation. A print by Jon Salway of 1985 sets Cleaver's image with ironical intention against a phrase quoted from Max Hastings, 'There is scarcely a man on the islands who does not think the price is worth paying', while Kit Edwardes and John Podpadec, in an installation piece commissioned by Manchester City Art Galleries, traced a genealogy of the aestheticization of explosions in nineteenth-century engravings of ships meeting the same fate as the *Antelope*; in photographs of shell bursts from the First World War, and in firework displays proclaiming triumphal moments of the Empire. In such images, the explosion as ejaculatory moment implicates the expression of male sexuality in an exercise of power whose ultimate embodiment is an act of annihilation.

If Cleaver's image of the *Antelope* has become a central focus for artists engaged in a critical examination of the underlying narrative of the war, then the anonymous photograph of the sinking *General Belgrano* has had an equally powerful hold over the imagination. The image both refers us to the specific historical moment and defeats it. It seems to come from another time – the very fact that the *Belgrano* was the ex-Second World War *USS Phoenix* coupled with the grainy texture of the photograph gives it a suspended quality of unreality. It could as easily have come from an old newsreel or even a movie. Like the photograph of the exploding *Antelope*, the sinking *Belgrano* gained the currency it did because it fitted with a recovered narrative of the past. The image excludes the immediate human tragedy of 368 men drowning in a hostile and freezing sea. Diana Constance recognized this effect when she produced a pastel drawing for the cover of *The Unnecessary War*.[16] Taking the image as characteristically cropped by the press (the photograph as supplied by Associated Press showed the *Belgrano* to be at a much greater remove from the camera), she showed the silhouette of the cruiser under an icy and bloodshot sky; the domes of the life-rafts in the foreground of the source photograph replaced by enormous swells sucking under pale and ghostly bodies.

Fig. 12   Michael Sandle, *Medal of Dishonour* (1986). (By kind permission of the artist.)

Michael Sandle reworked the theme in a very different context – one rarely employed by contemporary fine artists – the commemorative medal (Fig. 12). Cast in bronze in shallow relief it shows the *Belgrano* surrounded by drowning figures; in the centre a laurel-wreathed death's head spews out serpents and is encircled by the Latin inscription *Imperatrix impudens* ('the shameless Empress'). The medal is the élite elder cousin of the coin of the realm. The images which it carries celebrate the symbols of the state's power and its moral authority in an hieratic mode where design elements can only change to a limited degree within certain strictly defined and 'classical' parameters. This is clear in the 'Falklands Task Force Crownmedal' (Fig. 13) struck to celebrate the victory and to raise money for the South Atlantic Appeal Fund (a charity set up to help the injured and the relatives of those killed or maimed in the war). In contrast to the 'finely frosted reliefs set against mirror-brilliant backgrounds', Sandle's medal has a dark matt patina and is roughly textured in a manner more suited to the full-scale public war memorial. By inserting this mode into the aesthetic discourse of the traditional medal, it intensifies and lends support to the use of the medal form as a site of protest. No wonder that the Worshipful Company of Goldsmiths tried to have it banned!

Contribute to the
SOUTH ATLANTIC FUND
FALKLANDS TASK FORCE
CROWNMEDAL®

Fig. 13 Falklands Task Force crownmedal (advert).

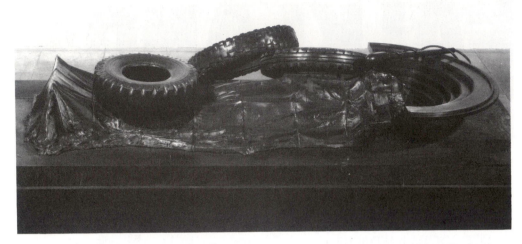

Fig. 14 Michael Sandle, *Caput Mortuum: A Commentary* (1983). (By kind permission of the artist.)

Sandle's other Falklands bronze, *Caput Mortuum: A Commentary* (1983) (Fig. 14), is cast on the scale of the public memorial and makes evident reference to the recumbent figure from Charles Sargent Jagger's *Royal Artillery Memorial* (1921–25) at Hyde Park Corner. Jagger's sculpture, which Sandle admires, introduced a concept of physical strife and sacrifice without the allegorical baggage which had previously been the norm. Sandle's 'memorial' takes this idea and places it in an oppositional context – suggesting not sacrifice but waste. A shrouded and decaying corpse is weighed down against the weather by tyres placed at random, while the gagged mouth of the skull is offered a microphone from atop an element shaped like a neo-classical amphitheatre. These elements allude to the power/knowledge construct of the modern state, its coercive control of and through the media and its semblance of order, while the crumpled drape of the tarpaulin and the abandoned tyres suggest its collapse. As Jon Bird, in an excellent analysis of Sandle's work puts it:

> . . . during periods of conflict – war, revolution, social unrest and civil disobedience – it is dirt that signifies the rupture of social and political definitions: the rubble of the barricade and the waste-ground, the debris that remains after bombardment, the discarded junk that marks the moment of retreat.[17]

Graham Ashton, one of Sandle's erstwhile pupils, has explored other

Fig. 15   Graham Ashton, *Lifeboat, Ha!* (1983) and *Fascio/Fiasco* (1983). (By kind permission of the artist.)

possibilities for a critical form of commemorative sculpture. While in grand public sculptures from the Renaissance to the early twentieth century, classical mythology, its order and permanence, were constantly invoked to support the ideology of the state, Ashton in his boat sculptures, *Lifeboat, Ha!* (1983) and *Fascio/Fiasco* (1983) (Fig. 15) from the series *Dumb Reminders* (1983–84),[18] uses it to opposite ends or subverts its meanings. The two boats were part of a convoy of five but conceived of as a separate pair and originally entitled *Fascio/Lifeboat (1200.23.5.1982)* in reference to the time and date when the *Antelope* was struck by Argentinian bombs. The sarcastic exclamation of the title *Lifeboat, Ha!* is reinforced materially by the boat's construction from cast concrete. The mooring pole placed across a concrete lifebelt and the coins scattered across the bottom of the boat refer to classical mythology: Charon, who ferried the souls of the dead across the River Styx received payment for each corpse in the form of a coin placed in its mouth. The work is an elegiac meditation on the wasted lives of the Falklands War, on the nature and meaning of sacrifice, and on the memorial sculpture as a mythologized rite of passage bound up with the rhetoric of nationhood. While *Lifeboat, Ha!* utilizes mythological narrative reflectively and ironically, *Fascio/Fiasco* explodes it in angry condemnation of its uses by the state – both historical and contemporary in reference to the Falklands. The ancient symbol of the *fasces* which stood for the authority of Roman law and connects the piece with the classical theme of *Lifeboat, Ha!*, is subverted along with its extensions of meaning in history. Where the rods of the *fasces* are frequently shown tied around the axe as a symbol of military and state power, Ashton replaces this with a phallic torpedo which smashes sideways through the faggots. Ashton not only offers analyses of ideology through his use and subversion of symbolic elements, but reclaims the aesthetics of form and surface to this function by using blood-red paint and a black latex rubber surface on the boat to suggest the resultant suffering of the burned and the maimed as the cost of militaristic rhetoric.

Among painters dealing with the ideological terrain of warfare, Paul Gough works in a manner close to that of Sandle and Ashton. His work is an attempt to create a history painting for the 1980s on an appropriately ambitious scale. It deals with the contemporary political worked through the allegorical, literary and mythological. In *Deluge* (1987–88) (Fig. 16), the work is dominated by a figure clad in medieval armour which stands for the 'blind power' of state force. It embodies the recovered image of the Armada and the chivalric crusading spirit imparted to the Task Force by the media which is symbolically represented as hands made from newsprint caressing the armoured figure. About its waist the figure carries a rusted and burning hulk symbolizing both the loss of ships and the war's subtext of the declining power of the Navy within the hierarchy of the conventional forces. Standing astride the parapet of 'Fortress Falklands' the figure is surrounded by that signifying detritus which Sandle incorporates into his sculpture, while in the background Gough quotes devices from Vorticism, which in the years leading up to the First World War developed an aesthetic of violent dynamism and liberation through conflict. Thus Gough implicity comments on a moment in British art where aesthetic radicalism set itself in opposition to the norm through a form of right-wing and militaristic rhetoric rather than through social concerns.

The work discussed so far has fallen into the category of artistic production intended for eventual consumption by a viewing audience possessing the requisite 'cultural capital', whether in galleries or in private homes. With the exception of Linda Kitson's drawings, much of what has been produced uses the Falklands as a focus for oppositional statements to the Thatcher government made in the belief that art can have some form of direct political affect (although this was, in view of the fact that much of it was made after the event, framed in a general sense and not in specific relation to the conflict itself). In this respect, cartoonists in the press and the politically committed postcard makers at Leeds Postcards (from a socialist perspective) and South Atlantic

Fig. 16   Paul Gough, *Deluge* (1987–88). (By kind permission of the artist.)

Souvenirs (from an anarchist perspective) were far more successful in being able to create pertinent images while the war was being fought.

I now want to examine two areas of artistic production which fall outside the normal framing definitions for discussion of fine art: on the one hand, marine and military painting of the kind which appears in officers' messes, in the collection of the Fleet Air Arm Museum or reproduced in books celebrating the deeds of individual companies and fighting units; on the other, and in complete contrast, work produced by serving officers and ordinary seamen during therapy for post-traumatic stress disorder at the Royal Naval Psychiatric Hospital.

Military interest in, and praise for, a certain form of genre realism which reconstructs scenes of battle or concerns itself with the accurate rendition of the finest technical details of matériel has a long history. At the end of the First World War, Lieutenant-Colonel A. C. McLean was in charge of the commissioning of war artists to record the newly formed RAF and was on the General Committee of the Imperial War Museum. However, he was motivated primarily by a desire to further the prestige of the service and was determined only to appoint artists who were actually serving with the RAF because he believed that they would be best placed to provide the degree of technical accuracy he sought.[19] This attitude to the relationship between artists and the Armed Forces continued in the Second World War and persists today. In his foreword to *The Making of a War Artist, David Cobb: The Falklands Paintings*,[20] Admiral of the Fleet Lord Lewin describes the encouragement given to midshipmen to illustrate their journals with sketches as part of a tradition of topographical renditions of coastlines within the Navy[21] and adds that, 'Sailors have always been quick to discern and appreciate the skill of those who can catch the sea in all its moods and *truthfully represent ships in all their forms*' (my italics). David Cobb is considered to be qualified to render the 'truth' of the war, 'by a combination of artistic achievement, professional under-standing and wide experience of war at sea', he has 'depicted and described great events in such a way that those who were there will say "That is exactly how it was".'

Having been interested in recording the Task Force on the dockside before it set sail, Cobb approached the Admiralty for assistance in getting to the Falklands once the war had ended. The request was granted and Cobb spent a week on the islands making topographical sketches and drawings of equipment in the time-honoured style. Subse-quently, these were used to reconstruct various events in commissions for P&O Ferries, 2 Para and other regiments. Cobb's paintings are given a form of Impressionist surface which serves to reinforce a read-ing implying that they were done before the subject but they are other-wise typical of the genre of dramatic reconstruction of warfare which has its roots in nineteenth-century battle art epitomized by Lady Butler. As a form of illustration they exhibit a degree of basic technical compe-

Fig. 17   Peter Archer, *Sgt. Ian McKay VC, Mount Longdon 11–12 June 1982* (1983). (By kind permission of the artist.)

tence but, as with other practitioners like Terence Cuneo and Peter Archer (whose work exhibits an even greater degree of topographical and temporal separation from events), they reimpose order on conflict through aesthetic and ideological means (Fig. 17). While purporting to represent the truth of the war, suffering, confusion, injury and death are elided and it is returned to the fantasy realm of *Boys' Own* comics. The inadequacy of these paintings is apparent as their signifying function exhibits a high level of redundancy in their closure around an ideology of unreflected heroic cause in the service of the state presented with the most uncomplicated of means. It is an ideology which fits with the simplistic narrative applied to the war by the press (discussed in more detail by James Aulich, Robert Hamilton and John Taylor in this volume).

Bearing in mind the lack of fit with historical reality apparent in illustrational military art, it might be instructive to compare Cobb's painting. *The Canberra's Return to Southampton* (1982) (Fig. 18), with McFadyen's representation of the returning Task Force. Cobb's view shows a collective order of naval might and the turning of the dockside welcome into a day of national flag-waving celebration, in contrast to McFadyen's emphasis on the event as an occasion for rabid nationalism and blood-lust. McFadyen's ideological position is as evident as Cobb's, but both paintings fail to deal with other orders of genuine experience

Fig. 18   David Cobb, *The Canberra's Return to Southampton* (1982). (By kind permission of the Fleet Air Arm Museum.)

associated with the homecomings. While these controlled public displays vindicated the state and its actions, they were also the medium for genuine and collective emotional release of tension on the part of those women who had suffered anxious waits throughout the war with little accurate information and who would soon be destined to return to their private lives to deal with the longer-term consequences.

The issue of the human cost of the war is a fraught one. The long-term damage can be as much psychological as physical; more so if one accepts Surgeon Commander Morgan O'Connell's estimate that for every combatant wounded in any given conflict there are three suffering from 'battle-shock'.[22] There is evidence that the military establishment as a whole has failed to recognize the full extent of post-traumatic stress disorder (PTSD) or even to recognize it at all, and there has been strongly voiced criticism from some quarters about the lack of assistance and aftercare available to Falklands veterans whose ability to lead a normal life has been seriously affected by the war even though they have no visible signs of injury (see Jeffrey Walsh, in this volume, on the films *Tumbledown* and *Resurrected*).[23] In this context, the Royal Navy has to be given credit for recognizing the existence of PTSD and for providing psychiatric care both during and after the conflict, although the rationale behind this raises a number of questions.

When the Task Force sailed for the islands, Surgeon Commander O'Connell from the Department of Psychiatry at the Royal Naval

Hospital at Haslar was on board the *Canberra* with the task of watching for signs of 'transient situation disturbance', as PTSD was defined by the International Classification of Diseases. Asked to define this by Polly Toynbee of *The Guardian*, O'Connell replied, 'an inability to fight which does not result from physical injury or disease'.[24] Military efficiency, and the need to keep as many men in the field as possible, was clearly the guiding principle behind the exercise. O'Connell was briefed to watch for early signs and then to remove men from the field for a rest period of 72 hours. In addition, however, O'Connell has provided therapy and aftercare beyond the period of the war itself. This has included an all important element of art therapy which has allowed patients to make forceful expressions of their experiences despite the limitations placed upon their means, both practical and ideological. Clearly the collages shown in Figs 19 and 20 have been directed in terms of their physical and compositional elements, but also in terms of a realignment of the identificatory process with their ships, with the Royal Navy and with a collectively acknowledged legitimation process in respect of the outcome of the war. O'Connell made clear the way in which the ideology of unquestionable service of state ends is implicated in military psychiatric practice. When asked by Toynbee what the diagnosis of one particular patient's illness was, O'Connell replied, 'Reactive psychosis':

PT: What is that?
MO: Losing touch with reality and a conflict of ideology.
PT: What sort of conflict?
MO: He had a strong feeling that the war should never have been allowed to happen. He could never manage to identify the Argentines sufficiently as enemies. He said he had no problems about the Russians but the Argentines were friends until a short time ago. He did see it was necessary to retake the Falklands but he thinks the invasion itself should have been prevented.

Bearing these factors in mind, it is possible to see the PTSD collages produced at Haslar as aids to a diagnostic process of reorientation where mental health is identified as the normative ground of military praxis to which the shocked and confused patient is successfully returned.

In the production of these collages, documentary records of the ships on which the patients have served are used as keys or points of identification from which more personal experiences can then be worked through. For instance, in one collage with *HMS Ardent* (Fig. 19), after being struck by bombs as the central focus, and a roll-call of the British Falklands dead encircling it, a picture of a gleaming *Ardent* in full-steam under a bright blue sky appears in the top right-hand corner as the point of identificatory reference which the patient strives to recon-

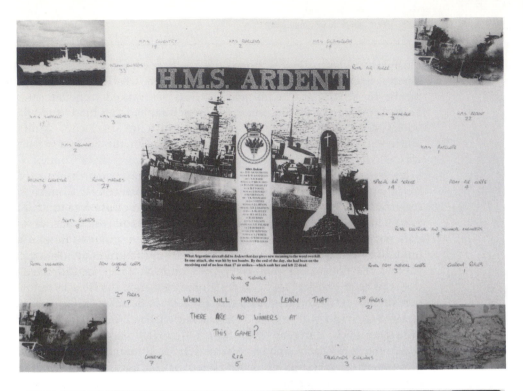

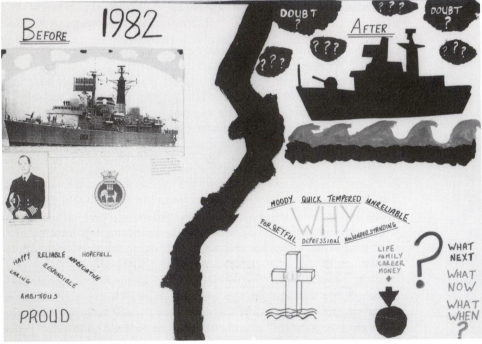

Figs 19 and 20   Collages produced by servicemen during post-traumatic stress disorder therapy at the Royal Navy Psychiatric Hospital, Haslor. (By kind permission of the servicemen.)

cile with subsequent events and to which he must return. As O'Connell stressed to Toynbee, the indoctrination process involves the creation of a bond between sailor and ship as symbolic entity such that its loss may be perceived as greatly as the loss of a colleague. The black-and-white photographs of the mangled stern and rear deck enveloped in acrid black smoke pull the focus of the narrative close in to the horror of the event and its traumatic memory.

In the bottom right-hand corner of the collage, a map is glued on. Maps embody a form of utilitarian knowledge in that they always bear some indexical relation to naturally existing forms, but this use value is always structured by what Jürgen Habermas calls an 'interest in prediction and control'; their value becomes apparent in relation to their function. Before the war, comparatively few people knew where the Falklands were on the globe, never mind what they looked like. So maps were necessary as an aid in the press and on television to a conception of the territory at stake. Large-scale maps were also utilized in briefing sessions to inform troops of the nature of the terrain to be fought over, plans for bridgeheads and the advancement of forces. But here, as in the media, they assumed a more subtle purpose. Repeated often enough alongside the rhetoric of their Britishness, they reinforced a process of identification with national territory which was symbolically conflated with the way in which the coastline of the British Isles is used as a signifier of national identity, history and destiny beyond its primary geographical function. With the use of the map of the Falklands in PTSD collages, something of this symbolic role and of the individual's part in achieving national aims is clearly intended. In other collages, the map is re-used in different ways but always stands in some way for a totalizing experience of the war (see Nick Caistor and James Aulich, this volume, for further discussion on the role of maps in the representation of the conflict).

Despite the level of ideological direction involved and their crude presentation, genuine and deeply moving feelings are clearly expressed. In another collage which deals with the sinking of *HMS Coventry*, the ship again appears top right as a grounding in better times (Fig. 20). The photograph is given a child-like and touching surround of blue sky, cotton wool clouds and a radiant sun to affirm this meaning. In the centre, an ugly black lightning strike cuts through this world and on the right the ship becomes a black silhouette surrounded by dark clouds filled with question-marks. Where the black line bisects the image, the collage is literally torn in two creating a painful and moving image of the chasm of experience which must be reconciled.

Where the media brushed aside the fact of the losses and terrible injuries or treated them with expressed concern (see John Taylor, this volume), they are always brought sharply to mind in these collages. The names are not those of anonymous participants as they appear in press accounts but friends and colleagues recalled by first name or nickname. Images of marriage break up and drink problems are often referred to by the unsettling slicing up or tearing of family snaps with drawings of walls or pictures of bottles inserted between the two halves. Against the odds, these images seize back the representation of the war from the cultural milieu of those who proposed to speak on the behalf of those who fought. Yet their access to a truth value beyond the personal is limited by the processes whereby all meaning is more or less socially determined.

Artistic production which concerned itself with the representation of the Falklands conflict was, then, bounded by the parameters set by the terms of the national rhetoric which surrounded the war and which constructed it as instant popular mythology. Access to the nature of the conflict on the ground which had been the determining characteristic of the art of the First and Second World Wars, was compromised both through internal considerations (moral choices about what to record in the case of Kitson) or through external directives. Most artists could only respond to the war critically and discursively through second-order discourses which examined pre-existing representations and then only where their practice encompassed or was specifically concerned with such strategies.

A new and entirely different situation of military confrontation faced the world in the Gulf. The determining power of the media in the shape of Cable News Network demonstrated an even greater degree of penetration into the course of history, not just controlling representation, but shaping potential conflict as spectacle. In this context, what possible role can there be for the unique cultural object? Clearly, the Artistic Records Committee of the Imperial War Museum still believes that one exists, as the artist John Keane was sent to the Gulf and even the figure of the war artist can become a cultural icon worthy of satire by a cartoonist like Steve Bell![25]

Notes

This essay is a revised version of 'We are All Falklanders Now: Representation, War and National Identity', which appeared in Aulich and Wilcox (eds) (1988). *The Falklands Factor: Representations of a Conflict*, exhib. cat., Manchester, Manchester City Art Galleries.

1 The Sunday Times Insight Team (1982). *The Falklands War: The Full Story*. London, Sphere, p. 233.
2 See Wright, P. (1985). *On Living in an Old Country*. London, Verso, pp. 1–27.
3 See Anderson, B. (1983). *Imagined Communities: Reflections on the Origins and Spread of Nationalism*. London, Verso, pp. 14–16. Anderson proposes that a nation is 'an imagined political community': 'It is *imagined* because the members of even the smallest nation will never know most of their fellow-members, meet them, or even hear of them, yet in the minds of each lives the image of their communion.' The nation 'is imagined as a *commun-*

ity, because, regardless of the actual inequality and exploitation that may prevail in each, the nation is always conceived as a deep, horizontal comradeship.'

4 Hood, V. T. (1989–90). Unpublished interview with Linda Kitson. I am grateful to Valda T. Hood for allowing me access to her interviews with Kitson, Leonard Rosoman and Angela Weight.

5 Ibid.

6 Kitson, L. (1982). *The Falklands War: A Visual Diary*. London, Mitchell Beazley, in association with the Imperial War Museum, p. 10.

7 Ibid., p. 41.

8 *Daily Mirror*, 4 November 1982.

9 All newspapers reported Kitson's descriptions of freezing rain, hail, violent winds and deep mud.

10 *Daily Express*, 4 August 1982.

11 *Daily Star* and *Daily Express*, 4 August 1982.

12 Vaizey, M. (1982). *Sunday Times*, 14 November.

13 For differing views of the effectivity of politically and socially directed art in 1980s Britain see Roberts, J. (1990). *Postmodernism, Politics and Art*. Manchester, Manchester University Press, pp. 57–117; Taylor, B. (1987). *Modernism, Post-Modernism, Realism*. Winchester, Winchester School of Art Press; (1987) *State of the Nation*, exhib. cat., Coventry, Herbert Art Gallery and Museum, and (1987) *Critical Realism*, exhib. cat., Nottingham, Nottingham Castle Museum.

14 Barthes, R. (1977). *Image–Music–Text*. London, Fontana, p. 25.

15 First published in *Jobs for a Change*, GLC Economic Policy Group (1983). Reproduced in Kennard, P. (1990). *Images for the End of the Century: Photomontage Equations*. London, Journeyman Press, unpaginated.

16 The Belgrano Action Group (1988). *The Unnecessary War: Proceedings of the Belgrano Enquiry November 7/8th 1986*. Nottingham, Spokesman.

17 Bird, J. (1988). 'The spectacle of memory'. In *Michael Sandle: Sculpture & Drawings 1957–88*, exhib. cat., London, Whitechapel Art Gallery.

18 Made during a year spent as artist in residence at the Walker Art Gallery, Liverpool 1983–84. See (1984) *Graham Ashton: Dumb Reminders*, exhib. cat., Liverpool, Walker Art Gallery.

19 See Harries, M. and Harries, S. (1983). *The War Artists*. London, Michael Joseph, p. 136.

20 (1986) Conway Maritime Press Ltd.

21 It is also worth noting the use made of sketches of the Falklands coastline drawn by Major Ewen Southby-Tailyour while sailing around the islands in 1978 in the assessment of landing sites for Operation Corporate (the codename for the re-taking of the Falklands). See The Sunday Times Insight Team, op. cit., note 1, pp. 106 and 177–8.

22 Toynbee, P. (1982). *The Guardian*, 1 November.

23 See Toynbee, P. (1983). *The Guardian* 21 November. Wade Tidbury in *The Unnecessary War*, op. cit., note 16, pp. 120–24; Carr, J. (1984). *Another Story: Women and the Falklands War*. London, Hamish Hamilton; Nasmyth, P. (1990). 'Once a soldier . . .', *Observer Magazine*, 10 June.

24 Op. cit., note 22.

25 See Hunt, R. (1990). 'The art of war', *The Sunday Correspondent*, 26 August; Steve Bell (1990). 'If . . .', *The Guardian*, September, 1991.

| 5 | Wildlife in the South Atlantic: Graphic Satire, Patriotism and the Fourth Estate

James Aulich

We don't want to fight, but by Jingo if we do.
We've got the ships, we've got the men, and the money too.

Notions of national identity play a crucial part in our understandings of ourselves as subjects within wider 'imagined' communities. But they are neither so self-evident nor so natural as they appear.[1]

In cartoon and graphic representations of the Falklands conflict, various national narratives were utilized and adapted to tell the history of the war in easily understandable ways. Cartoons dramatize events through familiar public figures and, to a lesser extent, allegorical symbols. Rudimentary linear perspectives articulate simple, declarative, stage-like compositions. Illusionist conventions are not usually appropriated to cartoons and they do not conform to 'realist' narratives like those found in artists' impressions made for newspapers and news broadcasts, which have stylistic affinities with action comic strips, pulp fiction covers and Second World War propaganda (see Tim Wilcox and Fig. 17). However, appearing week by week, day by day, cartoons are structured in 'historical' time and the telling of stories in orderly and predictable ways. Formally they are inconsistent, therefore, with the simultaneity of postmodern high-technology warfare and advanced communications.

Cartoon's 'humour' and 'iconoclasm' operates within journalistic institutions and is often self-consciously aware of its place in regimes of truth determined by factors other than journalism's 'objective' criteria. Indeed, analysis is complicated by the elaborate contexts to which it belongs: vying for attention with news, sports reporting, editorials, letters, fashion, women's pages, headlines, photojournalism, advertising, and so on. Meanings are constructed by these contexts: beginning with the medium and publication and ending with the two extremes of proprietorship and audience.

The Language of Cartoon

Unlike many other aspects of the production of news, the entertainment component in cartoon (its humour and familiarity) offers few problems. Cartoon is understood to educate and edify within an enlightenment tradition going back to Gillray, Rowlandson and Cruickshank, continuing into the twentieth century through figures like Low and Vicky. The tradition constructs the cartoonist as a voice of emancipated and liberal individualism uncorrupted by the institutions of state and capital. He or she seizes upon the dominant narratives and histories of the time and through image and caption exploits or confronts the ethical and moral vacuities of the modern bureaucratic state. Through the juxtaposition of figures of speech with historical events, the absurdities and disjunctures produced by the scientific rationalism of modern life are concealed or revealed. But the cartoonist's language has limits determined by a variety of factors besides individual temperament and preference, including ownership, market forces, journalistic practice and the political complexion of the publication.

The incarnation of cartoonists in the public imagination is comparable to the outsider status of the avant-garde artist. Although, broadly speaking, they neither use avant-garde techniques like montage, nor do they shock or outrage. Furthermore, cast in the role of a moral barometer of society and the powerful, cartoonists are perceived to be immune from the general ills of the journalistic community. They do not 'doorstep' or violate the privacy of individuals and their 'bias' can be excused through the strength of their graphic satire. The pervasiveness of this model within the profession is spoken for by their independence, a direct relationship with their editors and in preferential terms of employment.

As a measure of increasing proprietorial interference, spring 1982 was marked by the departure of Harold Evans from the *The Times*. With Rupert Murdoch, Robert Maxwell and later Tiny Rowland, the idea of a free press as an independent mainstream institution, uncontaminated by outside interests, was gone forever. Its corollary was the transformation of the reader from consumer to product. This was caused by advertisers consolidating their financial role to become the real media consumers. Nick Lloyd, the editor of the *Daily Express*, said, 'We don't want to brand our paper, we want to identify the badges that our audience seeks.' Or, as the managing director of the Mirror Group put it, 'We tried to stand up for the man in the street, but he wasn't really interested. Now we're about entertainment....'[2] The result was a narrowing in the breadth of opinion expressed in the press and a knowing acceptance of distortion and fabrication in the manufacture of news. Fortuitously and controversially, these conditions proved extremely useful to the state during the conflict.[3]

Two examples are worth considering in relation to the range of

Fig. 21 Gerald Scarfe, 'We shall fight until the bitter compromise', *The Sunday Times*, 11 April 1982. (By kind permission of the artist.)

opinion expressed. The first is the reception of US Secretary of State General Al Haig's peace shuttles.[4] In cartoon, the Argentinians, in the person of their President General Galtieri or their Foreign Minister Costa Mendez, are rarely represented in negotiations. When present, they appear as comic combatants, as in Gerald Scarfe of the *Sunday Times*, 'We Shall Fight until the Bitter Compromise!' (11 April 1982) (Fig. 21) or as a literal sideshow in world affairs in Les Gibbard of *The Guardian*'s 'Sniff! Sniff! Al, do you smell burning?' (23 April 1982) (Fig. 39). While Haig's role was widely perceived as marginal or passive, if not simply irritating. Wally Foulkes as Trog of *The Observer* depicts him as a tremulous dove of peace approaching a disapproving Thatcher-as-Nelson's-column (25 April 1982); Gibbard becalms him in a dinghy as the aircraft carrier *HMS Westminster* steams past (15 April 1982) and Mac of the *Daily Mail* had him asleep in the cabinet room suffering from jet-lag (13 April 1982). Nicholas Garland of the *Daily Telegraph* and Scarfe scatter peace proposals in the seas of the South Atlantic. Within such representations, ironic or not, negotiations are never a serious option and the reader is prepared for their imminent failure.

The second is the depiction of the islanders. One of the government's primary sticking points in negotiations, aside from the issue of sovereignty, was the self-determination of the islanders. Events prevented any practical assessment of the 'paramount wishes' of the Falklanders and in reporting and in cartoon they are, to all intents and purposes, absent. When the islanders do appear, they are most often represented as sheep (in Low's cartoons of the 1930s, the common people of the world). They are iconographically unsuitable for anything other than victims –

as incapable of self-determination as lambs to the slaughter. The illustrator Raymond Briggs does give them serious consideration in his moral tale *The Tin-Pot Foreign General and the Old Iron Woman*. Published as a book in 1985, it was far removed from the formal constraints of the daily press both temporally and institutionally. He represented the islanders as simple shepherds, freeborn Englishmen living in liberty until they are interfered with, first, by the Argentinian and then the British Armed Forces. Eventually, they return to their original pastoral state, their material conditions devastated under the rhetorical weight of the Iron Lady and the Tin-Pot General.[5]

What was at stake for parliament and the press, it seems, were questions of national sovereignty, pride and vulgar patriotism, rather than the fate of the islanders. On the day *The Guardian* reported President Reagan's comment that Mrs Thatcher 'wants a skirmish', it published the views of Mr Edmund Carlisle from the Falklands, brother of the former secretary of state for education: 'The majority of the Falklands people do not want Britain to take military action. People's

Fig. 22 Bill Caldwell, 'We're expecting a big crowd later', *The Star*. (Express Newspapers plc.)

attitudes have changed dramatically. We are prepared to consider Argentine sovereignty over the islands in return for withdrawing the troops.' Likewise, the woman who ran the pub and store in Port Stanley was quoted as saying, 'it will be great if the Argentinians bring newspapers, television and radios which we have not had before'.[6] But such views were almost entirely exceptional. Interestingly, Keith Waite of the *Daily Mirror* drew an Argentine soldier serving a curfew on a group of islanders, 'You mean you expect us to give up night clubs, discos, dog racing, the opera, the theatre?' (30 April 1982), as an ironic comment on the frugality and material barrenness of the islanders' lives. But Bill Caldwell of the *Daily Star* was more predictable with 'We're expecting a big crowd later' (June 1982) (Fig. 22), as the landlady of the Port Stanley Arms lines up the pints in anticipation of the arrival of the British forces.

The cartoonist does not influence or create opinion, but identifies marketable positions within dominant liberal, conservative and populist orthodoxies constituted in the media: the *Daily Star* is supportive of armed conflict, the *Daily Mirror* more sceptical. As a register of the diversity of public opinion, the press is a very unreliable indicator unless we are prone to accept it alone is capable of producing opinion. It has long been recognized that popular sentiments are subject to the freedom of the marketplace: the point about the production of news is that it is predetermined by those (the 'chattering classes') who have access to the producers (the 'deciding classes'). Combined with the influence of proprietors, advertisers and government, independent opinion tends to be restricted to differences between factions of the powerful. By these means, political realities and possibilities are shaped and defined at the expense of their determination in everyday life.

War as Sport, Sport as War

The Falklands campaign began with the run up to the World Cup Football competition and journalists and cartoonists alike lost no time in mediating the life and death affairs of warfare with the drama of the playing field and its myths of national superiority and individual heroism. Even before the invasion, the slogan *Las Malvinas son Argentinas* appeared at football matches in Argentina;[7] after the occupation, one widely reproduced Argentinian cartoon published in the British press featured their World Cup mascot with the map of the Falklands under his arm and his foot on the British Lion; and, later, Admiral Woodward described the voyage to the islands as 'the run up to the big match which in my view should be a walkover'.[8]

Sport's metaphorical currency frequently led to the portrayal of the common soldier's understanding of the war in terms of football. In this way, war is made safe for the reader. Crucially, sport is controlled, it has its seasons, its rules, even its field of conduct where a cast of heroes and villains enact successes and failures in the noble quest for victory. Its narratives are conventional and nostalgic and have associations with the vacuity of English aristocratic and upper middle-class sentiment (exposed in cartoon by David Low of the *Evening Standard* in the 1930s with the figure of Colonel Blimp); working- and lower middle-class images of national character like 'Tupper of the Track' of the boys' comic *The Rover* and the real life media constructions of hardy tenaciousness found in the figures of Steve Ovett and Steve Cram.

Trog, for example, portrays soldiers from both sides thinking of the battle to come as a World Cup match, as if, in some way, the conflict was indeed an abstract contest of national honour.[9] Gibbard plays on the old generals' exhortation, in the interests of discipline and morale, to dribble a football through No Man's Land. But here the football of the United Nations Organization (UNO) emblem bounces alone while the war cabinet stay in their entrenched position (26 April 1982). They are less gentlemanly and more pragmatic than the old stereotype allows. The eternal values of the 'Golden Age' of English sport appeal less than self-interest. By 1982, the type had lost some of its gloss, stereotypically, England had relinquished its status on the world stage as a major player and worse still could not any longer be sure of defeating 'inferior' Third World nations at football.

Sport's narratives of unreflective masculinity stand in stark contrast to the implausibility of heroic fantasy in modern high-technology warfare. Its vocabulary is emotional and sometimes almost hysterically chauvinist and it lends itself to a telling of the war that owes more to the gut than the intellect, as headlines like 'We'll beat them at Soccer too!' amply illustrate.[10] But such representations mystify as Waite points out in his cartoon of beleaguered Argentinian soldiers celebrating the broadcast: 'and here is our first World Cup Football result ... Argentina 79 Belgium 0' (15 June 1982) (Fig. 23); in fact, they lost 1–0. Tales of derring-do, dazzling performance and rugged professionalism in the national cause provided one of the ways the war gave substance and news-worthiness to the rhetoric of 'Thatcherism', summed up in Prime Minister Margaret Thatcher's Cheltenham address of 3 July 1982:

> When we started out there were waverers and the fainthearts, the people who thought we could no longer do the great things we once did, those who believed our decline was irreversible, that we could never again be what we were, that Britain was no longer the nation that had built an empire and ruled a quarter of the globe.

All too often, however, the representation of the Falklands conflict with its historical memories of imperial grandeur degenerated into a rampantly patriotic and xenophobic nationalism. It produced a 'Falklands' culture as one of the familiar constructions of sporting life in the

Fig. 23 Keith Waite, '. . . and here is our first World Cup Football result . . . Argentina 79 Belgium 0', *Daily Mirror*, 15 June 1982. (By kind permission of the artist.)

1980s. The journalist Ed Vuillamy wrote of the Heysel Stadium disaster in 1985:

> their drunken, blood-thirsty and racist English 'honour' that the terraces be cleared of 'Spiks' and the Union Jack flown unchallenged. I saw one Liverpool fan with a T-shirt: 'Keep the Falklands British' as though he and his mates were the task force. Perhaps, as he kicked and punched, he thought, in the *Sun*'s infamous screech of violent chauvinism 'GOTCHA!' ... Indeed, there was little to differentiate the drunken hysteria in the bars of Brussels and one night in a packed pub in Tufnell Park in 1982, when gleeful patriots celebrated the sinking of the *Belgrano* in a wash of beer: the drinkers looked alike and the tunes were the same – the words adapted. Politicians and sociologists can argue about whether the behaviour of these fans is legitimised by the patriotism currently preached by the leaders of society – but the important point is that the fans think it is.... In this way violence is made heroic in national life.[11]

Stanley Franklin of *The Sun*'s Ten ... Nine ... Eight ... Seven ... Six' (30 April 1982) (Fig. 24) typifies this discourse of jingoistic

Fig. 24   Stanley Franklin, 'Ten ... Nine ... Eight ... Seven ... Six', *The Sun*, 30 April 1982. (By kind permission of Kelvin McKenzie of *The Sun* newspaper.)

nationalism and demonstrates its dependence on racial stereotypes. A frightened, diminutive gaucho, complete with poncho, sombrero and handlebar moustache squats on the islands surrounded by the might of the Royal Navy arranged in the emblematic pattern of the Union Jack. Like Manuel, the Spanish waiter in *Fawlty Towers*, he is congenitally stupid and always a victim: anxious, emotional, unthinking, ineffectual, suggestible, dependent and weak. In contrast to the masculinity of the hooligan, the Latin is utterly feminized. While the type had many comparisons in the media, its closest heirs were found in the propaganda cartoons by the Royal Marine Illustrators Warrant Officer Roy Carr, Colour Sergeant Arthur Huddart and Sergeant John R. Webb, where large, physically strong Marines habitually flatten the small, physically weak Latin foe.[12] The stereotype partakes of a Second World War discourse of Latin cowardice in the popular construction of the Italian war effort. As such it is highly potent and it was considered sufficiently important for morale to rush editions to the Task Force in the first two weeks of the conflict.

Hooligan behaviour is condemned by the press and the government yet it is legitimized by the shared aggressive rhetoric of 'standing up for Britain'. Some cartoonists like Franklin gloried in their violent reputation with 'Run for your lives! Pym's dropping Aston Villa hooligans on us!' (23 April 1982); while Caldwell airlifts mods and rockers onto a Task Force carrier, 'The magistrate said: "If you want a punch-up go to Port Stanley beach – not Southend"' (13 April 1982). Celebrated because of their penchant for maverick and spirited behaviour, this patriotic type is related to the British bulldog, companion of John Bull, the essence of English popular independence.[13] But first and foremost the hooligan was a symbol of 'might is right', Argentinian or British. Cummings of the *Sunday Express* portrayed Thatcher, wearing a Union Jack vest, as the accused in the world court, facing the Argentinian hooligan prosecution witness in front of the multi-racial UNO jury: 'Prisoner in the dock! You are accused of giving a black eye to this skinhead when he mugged you! (8 May 1982) (Fig. 25). The popular papers and the majority of the Members of Parliament appealed to a jingoistic collectivity they would not admit to. The hooligan as a target for criticism was made in their own image: 'The jingo is the aggregation of the bully. An individual may be a bully: but, in order to create jingoism, there must be a crowd.'[14]

The hooligan has stuck as an image of chauvinist national state aggression and has characterized constructions of nationalist sentiment throughout the 1980s. A more recent cartoon by Trog shows Thatcher, her patriotism transformed from the godlike regality of Britannia, to the simple chauvinism of the football hooligan sporting a Union Jack T-shirt stomping all over Jacques Delors, President of the European Commission (8 July 1990).

Fig. 25 Cummings, 'Prisoner in the dock! You are accused of giving a black eye to this skinhead when he mugged you!', *Sunday Express*, 8 May 1982. (Express Newspapers plc.)

National Histories

Steve Bell of *The Guardian* set out a dissenting position with his character Kipling (Fig. 26). Bell's work belongs to a distinctive tradition, originally divorced from the mainstream, and characterized by the 'underground' work of Robert Crumb on the one hand, and the mischievous anarchy of *The Beano*'s 'Desperate Dan' and the 'Bash Street

Fig. 26 Steve Bell, 'If . . . This is really too bad, Kipling! Why are you engaged in this barefaced treachery??', *The Guardian*, 16 April 1982. (By kind permission of the artist and The National Museum of Labour History, Manchester.)

Kids' on the other. In both instances, his style is divorced from the 'heroics' of many orthodox strips and signifies an anarchic and oppositional stance of liberal scepticism.

Kipling is based on the figure of the gallant common sailor, Jack Tar, who had emerged in the popular theatre of the early nineteenth century as a proletarian hero. 'Always on terms of easy familiarity with his captain, or mutinous',[15] he is a symbol of nautical power and fair play whose liberal conscience causes nothing but trouble. So defined, he personifies a body of opinion in the *The Guardian*'s readership also found among the Armed Forces, many of whom resented engagement in what they regarded as a politicians war. Lieutenant David Tinker RN wrote:

> I cannot think of a single war in Britain's history which has been so pointless.... This one is to recapture a place which we were going to leave undefended from April, and to deprive its residents of British citizenship in October. And to recapture it, having built up *their* forces with the most modern Western arms.[16]

As a body of opinion it never gained much currency so far as it is possible to tell from either the MORI polls, that registered increasing support for armed action as the campaign proceeded, or the press in general. Thought and attitudes, it seems, were kept within acceptable bounds.

Some of the most virulent criticism of government action came from Rick Walker and Steve Hardstaff of South Atlantic Souvenirs (Fig. 27), a postcard company with outlets in the 'alternative' sector:

> we were quite apprehensive about the reception the cards would get. They seem mild enough now, but the tide of hysteria whipped up by the tabloids made me, at least, worry that if we were identified we might get attacked in our homes ... [but] ... as far as selling cards went, we did better than our wildest dreams, selling out the first print run completely in a few weeks.[17]

The expression of pacifist and anarchist sentiment was felt to be dangerous. Yet, there was a ready market that remained largely unexploited by the mainstream press.[18]

More acceptable, but in many ways no less critical of government policy, was the homely, comfortable, reassuring and almost unbearably familiar world of Carl Giles in the *Sunday Express*. Bell summed up its ethos in the invention of the Penguin, a natural inhabitant of the South Atlantic but somehow resolutely British: 'It's given me a reason to carry on through this madness', cries Kipling. It stood for memories of a 'Pick up a Penguin' chocolate-biscuit-universe of innocent and uncomplicated wish-fulfilment; the slightly ridiculous nostalgia of dinner suits and formal waiters; the dignified welfare statism of a self-educated generation nourished on Penguin Books; and the resolute international mod-

Fig. 27   South Atlantic Souvenirs, 'Let's Go Over the Top with the Tories: 255 Reasons Not to Vote Conservative' (1982). (By kind permission of Rick Walker.)

ernity and anachronistic domestication of the penguin pool at London Zoo. An ethos whose contradictions Bell confronts as the Penguin reveals himself to be a fifth columnist working for the European Economic Community (EEC) and when Kipling at last teaches it to speak English when it utters the word 'Rejoice!' (25 May 1982), as a reference to Thatcher's verdict to the press on the retaking of South Georgia (Fig. 26).

Giles, however, depicts a cameo of suburban life with all of its inertia, divisions, incomprehensions, indifferences, chauvinisms and provincialisms. It is the same deep-rooted and affectionate stereotype of English life exploited by the producers of situation comedies like Johnny Speight's *Till Death do us Part* and is distinct, say, from the more controversial *Boys from the Blackstuff* by Alan Bleasdale. He represents the little islander mentality found in the popular construction of a Churchillian England. Its vista extends from the domestic certainties of working- and lower middle-class suburbia to the Blimpish environs of a jaded upper class. There is no room for the stereotypes of the stark realities of the 1980s, with its instabilities, uncertainties, successes and transformations. Class conflict and political militancy is no more than

Fig. 28 Giles, 'But when the blast of war blows in our ears ... Stiffen the sinews, Summon up the blood ... Clear out the old air-raid shelter', *Sunday Express*, 3 April 1982. (Express Newspapers plc.)

bar room banter, the yuppie a spectre on a distant horizon. Even Gran'ma's reversion to a Second World War mentality raises nothing more than quiet scepticism among her community (Fig. 28). However, her mood struck a national chord summed up in a *Sunday Telegraph* editorial of 30 May 1982:

> People look back nostalgically to the time in 1940 when all classes joined together in a common purpose, transcending sectional or class divisions [Gran'ma tells the upper classes to get their Union Jack the right way up (11 May 1982)].... Up to a point during recent weeks, these prayers have been answered. ... How long will this new mood last? ... new generations made aware of the strength of their patriotism ... discipline, sacrifice, gallantry, duty and professional excellence.

Old certainties were marshalled to an unstable present. The day after Parliament voted to despatch the Task Force on 3 April 1982, Gran'ma clears out the air raid shelter while a bemused younger generation read of a 'Falklands Farce'. But Giles' quiet scepticism was out of temper with the editorial line of his newspaper which the day before had

Menendez 'usurping the wartime Spitfire pilot Rex Hunt' (the Governor of the Falkland Islands); the 'flag hauled down by an inferior power', and the Falklanders 'wholly British in origin, sentiment and loyalty, to remain British and to continue to live under British rule must be defended as if it were the Isle of Wight which had been invaded'. Such simple caution, if it were felt by elements of the wider population, was soon immersed in a current of chauvinism.

The English popular imagination is shot through with a rich strain of Romanticism that cartoonists of various persuasions tapped with enthusiasm. It is married to memories of naval supremacy aided by the fictional swash buckling of C. S. Forester's novels, Errol Flynn's films and the school textbook heroics of Francis Drake, the Duke of Wellington, Admiral Nelson and the spirit of Dunkirk. The rhetoric and discourse of the Second World War proved especially irresistible and even *The Guardian* reported on 17 April 1982 'Nazi scientists "helping" Argentina build Plutonium Plant'. Part of this discourse of 'Englishness' is a 'natural' aversion to military dictators, immortalized by Low in the 1930s and 1940s with Hit, Muss and Muzzler.[19] General Leopoldo Galtieri, President of Argentina, was really too good to be true for the media as a 'tin-pot' dictator of a Third World country 'well-known' for sheltering Nazis and criminals. Such representations had a dual effect. On the one hand, they compounded the limitations of the understanding of the history of the Argentinian people and the immediate dispute. On the other, they allowed for the war to assume a world significance it did not have, despite the government's claims to the contrary. Franklin, for example, situates the conflict within this version of national history of victory over tyranny as the 'British Demolition Company' swings into action over the caption 'Business as Usual' and knocks Napoleon, Bismarck, Mussolini, Hitler and Galtieri from their pedestals (21 June 1982). Conventionally, these versions of British history neglect to mention the international dimensions of Waterloo, the Somme and Allied victory in the Second World War. The generals variously represented as drunk, stupid or vain were most effectively lambasted on their civil rights record. Cummings' 'Ah! Senors, that's better! It's much better to stick to shooting our OWN people!' (18 June 1982), and Ralph Steadman's general feeding an infant the barrel of an automatic rifle,[20] are typical, referring to the inhumanity of the 'Dirty War' waged by the generals between 1976 and 1979. However, these stereotypes neglect the fact that Galtieri had taken office in 1981 with never fulfilled policies of slow political liberalization, a gradual return to democracy and the promise of information on the 'disappeared'.

As Thatcher became increasingly identified with the course of the conflict, so cartoonists clothed her as a military leader. But hers is not the disreputability of the dictator, but the moral authority of the defender of freedom and democracy. In her own words: 'we have a long and proud history of recognising the rights of others to determine their own destiny'. Cummings left no room for doubt with his representation of the prime minister as Lord Kitchener (15 April 1982), while Caldwell had her invading Europe in the face of EEC prevarication over sanctions against Argentina and the 'Victory' over farm prices exacted as their price (20 May 1982).

The rhetoric of the Second World War lent the conflict moral rectitude and obscured a number of problems. Certainly, government policy served notice on other undemocratic military states: but some islanders had requested evacuation; the question of sovereignty had been broached with the Argentinians in terms of lease back arrangements; and, in any case, how were democratic rights to be restored to a community which in large part did not have any? Gibbard hinted at some of the contradictions when he made a humanitarian statement with 'The price of sovereignty has been increased – OFFICIAL' (6 May 1982) (Fig. 29), in reaction to the decision to sink the *General Belgrano* and the Argentinian retaliation on *HMS Sheffield*. The cartoon is based on Zec's 'The price of petrol has been increased – OFFICIAL' (Fig. 30), originally published in the *Daily Mirror* in 1942 as a comment on the rising human cost of petrol at the time of U-boat attacks on Allied convoys. It attracted criticism from the government because of its potential effect on national morale, perhaps because its illusionist style invited realist interpretations and sympathy for the fate of the common sailor rather than the greater cause. In a conflation of patriotic zeal and market acuity, *The Sun* editorial of 7 May 1982 echoed the original attack on Zec's cartoon:

> There are no natural referees above the sound of the guns. A British citizen is either on his country's side – or he is its enemy.
>
> What is it but treason for *The Guardian* to print a cartoon, showing a British seaman clinging to a raft . . .
>
> Isn't that exactly calculated to weaken Britain's resolve at a time when lives have been lost, whatever the justice of her cause?
>
> Imagine a cartoonist who produced a drawing like that in Buenos Aires. Before he could mutter: 'Forgive me, Senors' he would be put up in front of a wall and shot.

As we have seen, Steve Bell also draws on seafaring narratives of national history; like Giles, he presents the reader with an independent world with a cast of characters largely independent of the political actors.[21] At the time of the Argentinian invasion, his characters were in Central America with 'a market research Task Force from Burgerqueen corporation'. But by 13 April 1982, the day after the 200-mile exclusion zone around the islands came into into operation, Bell created 'Jack Middletar Agent of Destiny'. The figure draws ironically on the ingenuous discourses of children's science fiction and the secret agent. Conceived as a parody of a Dan Dare-like figure, square-jawed and with fate on his side, his unquestioning loyalty takes him to faraway

Fig. 29 Les Gibbard, 'The price of sovereignty has been increased –
OFFICIAL', *The Guardian*, 6 May 1982. (By kind permission of the artist.)

Fig. 30 Zec, 'The Price of petrol has been increased by one penny –
OFFICIAL', *Daily Mirror*, 1942.

Fig. 31   Steve Bell, 'You know Kipling it's not every day your country wins a considerable victory . . .', *The Guardian*, 24 June 1982. (By kind permission of the artist and The National Museum of Labour History, Manchester.)

places in the eternal battle between good and evil. His alter-ego is the character Kipling whose name speaks for his delusions of imperial grandeur. Middletar, who could not quite sustain the 'High Tar' of *Player's Navy Cut*, commands the 'armoured nuclear punts' *HMS Incredible* and *HMS Amazing* (Fig. 31).[22] On the way to the South Atlantic, they come under 'Albatross attack'. The well-known symbol of the albatross, derived from memories of Samuel Taylor Coleridge's 'Rime of the Ancient Mariner' (1798), proved particularly apt as a source for a body of liberal opinion convinced of the folly of the operation, since the killing of such a portent of good fortune could only have fatal results.[23] Similarly, Peter Brookes utilized the bird as an expression of long-term scepticism in relation to British commitment (Fig. 32). As the historian E. P. Thomson remarked at the time:

> [There is] . . . something quixotic in this post-imperial nation with an ailing economy, to send out on three days notice 26,000 men and a vast armada to the opposite end of the oceans in defence of a few hundreds of its own nationals.[24]

On 21 April 1982, Martin Cleaver's photograph *Dawn over the South Atlantic aboard HMS Hermes* (Fig. 33) was widely published in the dailies as a register of the sublime technological heart of the military machine which would surely and efficiently arbitrate the natural course of the war should it come to a fight. Significantly, Bell featured Thatcher speaking to Woodward: 'Why is there nothing more you can do Admiral?' To which he replies, 'Madam, I'm sure you're aware of the repercussions if we actually sink anything?' It was a repetition of Kipling's foreboding remark of 16 April 1982, the day after the Argentine fleet left Puertas Belgrano: 'Face facts commander! We're on a hiding to nothing here!! Think of the consequences if we actually sink something!!' Implicit in such narratives is the inevitability of armed

Fig. 32 Peter Brookes, cover design for *The Listener*, 17 June 1982. (By kind permission of the artist and the Imperial War Museum.)

Fig. 33 Martin Cleaver, *Dawn over the South Atlantic on board HMS Hermes.* (Press Association.)

action and by 3 May 1982, with the sinking of the *Belgrano* and a few days later the *Sheffield*, references to the discourse of the romantic history of British naval supremacy come thick and fast. Franklin, for example, has the figure of Lord Nelson labelled 'Heroic Navy Spirit' cast the wreath 'Tribute to *HMS Sheffield*' on the waters of the South Atlantic (6 May 1982).

Frequently, the prime minister was identified with figures from national history. Cummings, for example, drew her as Queen Elizabeth I in a reference to the period when England first came of age as a nation with, as it so happens, a resolute woman at its head. More often, however, she was Wellington or Nelson, reincarnated triumphal personifications in English history and at odds with, say, William Lovett's recollections of Trafalgar and Waterloo as 'a black record ... of blood and human wretchedness'. Scarfe reduced the identification to farce with 'American Tourist Season Opens – Gee – I admire your National Monument'. Ronald Reagan as Mickey Mouse regales Thatcher as Nelson's Column but, humour aside, one national myth confronts another and to paraphrase Jean Baudrillard, the French philosopher: the real is not only what can be reproduced, but that which is already reproduced. The cartoonist's critical stance is complicit with imaginary structures of national and historical supremacy. Bell comments on the phenomenon circumspectly as the mutinous Kipling, that alternative embodiment of Englishness, undergoes a sex change. In an inversion of the process taking place in the media, a symbol of national character (Bell's Kipling) becomes the prime minister: 'Incredible to Redundant ... we have entered a war zone and my crewman has turned transvestite' (1 May 1982).

Bell points to the fact that many of these symbols of national history function as part of a series of complex significations with no clear or single meaning independent of specific historical contingencies. The iconographical representation of the Task Force as the Armada transformed Latin humiliation into British victory; while its emblematic identification with aircraft carriers considered obsolete by the Ministry of Defence and associated in the public mind with *American* victories over the Japanese during the Second World War might seem equally anachronistic.

Ironies like these were not lost on cartoonists especially in the light of the US and Britain apparently emerging as the senior partners of the NATO alliance in the embrace of the 'Special Relationship'. The latter was put under considerable strain because of US Latin America Policy, which leant widespread support to Argentina and other right-wing states in Southern and Central America, yet within the transcendent world order prescribed by Second World War narratives, Reagan could have little real choice which side he should support. It seems as if, Reagan, widely represented as an actor who might be expected to be duplicitous, or as an extremely skilful, if not entirely serious clown or

Fig. 34 Nicholas Garland, 'Clear the Decks', *Daily Telegraph*, 21 May 1982. (By kind permission of The Telegraph Group.)

acrobat, could hardly resist the power of a dominant popular rhetoric which represented him as a buddy, US Cavalryman or cowboy ready to provide aid in the cause of freedom and democracy.

National Leadership and the National Interest

One of the principal historical phenomena of the campaign was the means by which the person of the prime minister was identified with the national interest. The phenomenon was by no means restricted to the press but was found in the population at large if the opinion polls are to be believed. Just as Conservatism had appropriated the patriotism of John Peddie's mid-nineteenth-century urge to populist revolution, 'England expects every man to do his duty', so national identity fused with the values of an increasingly autocratic head of government and, in turn, was committed to the service of Conservatism. The iconography of war in cartoon makes this quite explicit. Gibbard depicts her, for example, as the figurehead of *HMS Westminster* in 'Sail and Steam' (15 April 1982); Garland portrays her as an able seaman sweeping the deck of an aircraft carrier of peace proposals, criticizing her resolve but at the same time inadvertently making common cause of War Cabinet policy, the desires of the military and the common man in 'Clear the Decks!' (21 May 1982) (Fig. 34); or straightforwardly by Cummings as

Fig. 35   Nicholas Garland, 'Nothing except a battle lost can be half so melancholy as a battle won', *Daily Telegraph*, 5 May 1982. (By kind permission of The Telegraph Group.)

a squaddie holding a Union Jack while assaulted by the vultures of UNO, EEC, Eire and Mr Benn(os) Aires as a header for Michael Toner's article 'At Stake – British Territory, British People and British Freedom' (23 May 1982).

National symbols like Britannia, for example, were often given Thatcher's features. Originally an antique personification iconographically associated with Britain as a colonial province of the Roman Empire, imperial ambition was a less significant association than popular resistance. From the seventeenth century, she symbolized the constitution and the protection of the people against the state: in James Thomson's eternal phrase, 'Britons never will be slaves', or as the Reverend Sydney Smith expressed it, 'What two ideas are more inseparable than Beer and Britannia'. As a patriot she was often conflated with Boadicea the warrior-queen and with the aid of Neptune's trident she dominated the unruly seas by strength of virtue. The warlike association was cemented in 1821 after Napoleon's defeat when she conventionally wore Athena's helmet. Her significance subtly shifted as defeat of foreign empire led to an inversion of emphasis and eventual identification with Queen Victoria, Imperial expansionism and a natural British world order.[25]

One variation of Britannia is the 'compassionate, weeping Madonna who mourns national tragedies and helps the afflicted'.[26] She appeared in this guise in Garland's cartoon of Britannia sitting on the barren landscape of the Falkland Islands amidst the wreckage of the *Belgrano* and the *Sheffield*, captioned by the Duke of Wellington's verdict after the battle of Waterloo, 'Nothing except a battle lost can be half so melancholy as a battle won' (5 May 1982) (Fig. 35). Through Britannia the British people were ascribed a humanitarianism by the cartoonist usually reserved for the prime minister alone, as in 'Her Private Agony' in *The Sun* of 6 May 1982. When identified with Thatcher, Britannia is no vulnerable virgin courted or threatened by greater powers, nor even the commanding nanny figure of the Victorian imagination, but a warrior-queen exhorting her people to battle against foreign tyranny. Scarfe's grotesque Britannia with sharp nose and gnashing teeth might speak for excessive zeal, but iconographically the figure of the prime minister is still conflated with a symbol of the British people and national identity within the discourse of an imperial mythology (20 June and 19 September 1982).

If there are any distinctions to be made beyond the immediate political biases of the individual cartoonists and publications, it lies in the degree of sophistication of the cartoon, so that, for example, David Hopkins' re-use of a 1854 cartoon from *Punch* as a design for the cover of *The Economist* (16–21 May 1982) (Fig. 36) makes a useful comparison with the Crimea. The original cartoon showed Lord Aberdeen struggling to restrain the British Imperial Lion (Fig. 37), but Hopkins replaces him with the prime minister and puts them both on the deck of a ship just off the Falklands coast. Alex Potts and Deborah Cherry commented:

> Indeed the crisis which brought Palmerston to power, the Crimean War, makes the most accurate historical parallel with Thatcherite militarism. Here, too, a fleet was launched ostensibly to teach a foreign aggressor a lesson by a show of Britain's Naval power. It was the first time the press played a major role in mobilising public opinion for a war effort.[27]

Whatever the opinion of the cartoonist, the prime minister's symbolic order is not just patriotic but 'natural', joined through the Lion to imperial ambition in the name of the people. The order was defined by Henry Kissinger in his speech to the Institute of International Affairs on 10 May 1982:

> Both Britain and America has [*sic*] learned that whatever their histories, their futures are part of the common destiny of freedom ... [we who] have contributed so much to the free world's unity and strength have another opportunity now, together with our

Fig. 36   David Hopkins, 'Let him go?', proof of cover for *The Economist*, 15–21 May 1982. (By kind permission of Ian Fleming Associates.)

Fig. 37   Lord Aberdeen restraining the British Lion, *Punch*, 1854.

allies, to show that the democratic nations are masters of their own destiny.

Steve Bell was unequivocal in his recognition of the rhetoric of the New Right in the 'Falklands Spirit' as he has Norman Tebbit regale the unemployed:

> Now you youngsters today are experiencing a crisis of values....
> The values that are traditionally held in highest regard – loyalty to family, church and crown ... have become undermined through years and years of flabby minded socialistic eyewash.... There's a straightforward solution to this essentially moral problem ... kill Pinko's Now (12 May 1982).

The Task Force was, in other words, endowed with missionary purpose in the protection of democracy in an extension of the cold war into the Third World, identifying the military regime with Communism as they made overtures to the USSR in the face of US sanctions. On the level of rhetoric, 'traditional values' were made substantial in the achievement of the Task Force regardless of the historical conditions which had enabled Britain to supply a third of Argentina's arms at the height of the 'Dirty War' and since then supplied ground attack aircraft to Suharto's Indonesia, courted the Shah of Iran and so on, all presumably in the name of democracy.

In this country and in the USA, 'Western Democracy' stood at the threshold of a 'welfare state for the privileged' and a significant extension of state power. In 1981, a much publicized meeting between Thatcher and Reagan was marked by talk of 'old certainties', 'true values', 'essential human qualities', 'destiny' and 'just cause' in defence of democracy. The Iron Lady seemed to have all the options of Churchill's rhetoric. In the face of a national humiliation brought about by a disreputable regime, the Conservative monopoly on patriotism, following the construction of a Conservative past from 1940 rather than Chamberlain's years of appeasement in the 1930s, easily led to an appropriation of the Left's moralism on a question of national sovereignty and the cause of anti-fascism: as Secretary of State for the Foreign and Commonwealth Office Francis Pym declared, 'Britain does not appease dictators'. Within the dominant rhetoric any vacillation in fulfilling fate's destiny was read as at best duplicitous, probably cowardly and at worst treasonous: Gibbard, for example, had Tony Benn, one of the major critics of armed conflict, heading for the escape hatch as the submarine *HMS Rejoice* sailed towards the darkening storm clouds ahead (27 April 1982).

Yet, for the Argentine Government, their actions were as honourable and were carried out in defence of Western values. The Argentine News Agency in the first half of April wrote of the invasion 'as the most historic event of the century' and an English language broadcast reported in the *Listener* (20 May 1982) said:

> Communism can make no progress when a country really asserts its national values and commands international respect. And this is precisely what Argentina is doing with regard to the *Malvinas*. We are therefore witnessing a rebirth of Argentine values and, simultaneously, of Western ideals in a part of the world which (as events have proved) is of great strategic importance now and in the future. Consequently, there is at this time no danger of foreign infiltration into the South Atlantic.... The new power which has become evident here in Argentina as from 2 April is Western by origin, situation and destiny. None renounces those ideals except those who betray them, and this is precisely what the British Prime Minister, Margaret Thatcher, and her government are doing.

So, unsurprisingly, in the Argentinian satirical magazine *Tal Cual*, Thatcher variously becomes a one-eyed pirate, a toothless witch, a 'Maldita' or 'evil speaker'. While Argentina's best-known cartoonist, Sabát (see Nick Caistor) of the quality daily *Clarin*, portrays her as an ageing, tarty, irrate, flabby and acquisitive housewife, supermarket trolley filled with arms; or, in profile, stooped and dejected, in a caricature taken from photograph of her leaving 10 Downing Street after the attack on *HMS Sheffield*. (The same event was documented in the British press with a photograph taken from the front, minimizing the hunched, almost crumpled posture of the prime minister.)

Satire in Argentina was a perilous business, contemporary Argentinian figures were criticized through personae drawn from the past to avoid censorship and probable persecution in a widely felt 'climate of fear'. The result was the development of complex allegories. A cartoonist for the weekly satirical magazine *Humor*, for example, has Costa Mendez catch a rodent-like Thatcher between the sheets with Admiral Massera, an early naval campaigner for the annexation of the islands and discredited member of the 1976 junta. Like eighteenth-century cartoon, they draw upon a discourse of patriarchal sexual libertinism as a measure of political inconstancy and corruption underwritten by more sinister undertones of domestic repression, torture and sexual violation. Sábat mixes contemporary with historical figures drawn from popular culture to represent Argentinian political life as a stage for a theatre of the absurd. His imagery relies for its effect on the mingling of low-life, sexual depravity and the quasi-criminal connotations of the tango and the night club where many former torturers had ensconced themselves.

Frequently, Sábat pictured British national ambition as an elderly weeping Queen Victoria. This was a rearticulation of attitudes which had considered Argentina little more than an outpost of Empire in the nineteenth century and had indirectly spawned anti-British nationalism and ultimately Galtieri's dictatorship. In Argentina, the policy of the British Government seemed less thoroughly identified with the figure of the Prime Minister. One cartoon in *Humor* shows John Bull exposing himself to the female personification of Argentina as a post-imperial obscenity desecrating her historical and republican credentials. But in Britain, as Garland illustrated in 'I can't see a damn thing' (16 May 1982), John Bull's English pedigree of pacifism (contrary to popular belief), anti-intellectualism, anti-heroism and victimization by the state proved an unsuitable carrier of a triumphant national identity that welded national interest to the values of a particular national leadership. Indeed, Argentinian cartoonists often perceived no distinction between British Government policy and the people as embodied in national histories personified by weeping and elderly Queen Victorias or vulgar and imperial John Bulls.

Casuists of Democracy

Perhaps one of the best documented aspects of the war is the relationship between the media, the government and the military. A free press is one of the foundation stones of any democracy and it is often used as a gauge of its success. However, the industry demands conformity within a system of public subsidy and private profit called free enterprise. A system, which according to Noam Chomsky, is subject to demands that would challenge, for example, 'excesses' of democracy where special interest groups express their views in opposition to dominant ideologies. These orthodoxies are determined by proprietorial and political interests related to issues of national security, good taste, domestic politics and what the government understood to be the dangers of reporting in an age of advanced communications.

A predominant feeling was that journalists were a peril for the defence of democracy and freedom and therefore could not be allowed to operate unchecked. As General Westmoreland said in spring 1982, 'I blame the news media for the erosion of support for our war. Vietnam was the first war fought without censorship, and without censorship things can get terribly confused in the public mind.' Subsequently, a journalistic memorandum condemned the handling of news by the Ministry of Defence using the '"figleaf of national interest to cover errors, omissions, muddle and lack of information", not to mention censorship, misinformation, delaying correspondents' reports and not allowing enough journalists to travel'.[28]

Once the Task Force had put to sea and the initial euphoria had died down, so the industry's biggest story began to dry up. A factor exaggerated by the control exerted on hard news. Like a football crowd at an uneventful match, the press began to pay more attention to itself than the war. A circulation battle developed with the popular papers competing to be the most patriotic in an identity of journalistic opinion, government policy and targeted market. Gibbard in 'Whoops a little boob there fans! See The Sun stop the knockers tit for tat!' (10 May 1982) (Fig. 38), has the two sides playing for the Falklands Cup. Thatcher the goalkeeper has let one past and the BBC, Financial Times, Daily Mirror and The Guardian photograph the error while the photographer from The Sun squirts water over them. Steve Bell commented on the phenomenon with a depiction of the press corps marching up and down the deck of HMS Redundant drilling with bottles of duty free to the chant 'Gung ho! Gung ho! Gung ho!' (20 April 1982), in contrast to Jak of the Daily Express', 'Right, gentlemen! How many of you can slide eighty feet down a rope from a helicopter?' as a challenge to their patriotism and assumed marketability in what was, by now, a growing assault on any view that might be seen to challenge the government or military.

As the tabloids engaged in their patriotic struggle and the broadsheets fought to preserve their ideological integrity as a fourth estate the war and its representation seemed to fuse. The media had become its own subject, endlessly reproducing itself, and as if to illustrate the point Garland, in a cover for The Spectator, shows the press, pen in hand, battling across the strife-torn landscape of the islands (22 May 1982). Consequently, the range of opinion on the war was reduced still further.

Fig. 38 Les Gibbard, 'Whoops a little boob there fans! See *The Sun* stop the knockers tit for tat!', *The Guardian*, 10 May 1982. (By kind permission of the artist.)

By 7 May 1982, sectors of the press were beginning to be criticized in the House of Commons for bias (see John Taylor, this volume). The BBC had included Argentinian footage and conducted interviews with MPs opposed to the war in a *Panorama* broadcast in a manner the MP John Page found 'totally offensive and almost treasonable'. The conservative press took up the cudgels with delight. Cummings, for example, features 'Traitorama' with the Kaiser, Hindenberg, Tirpitz and Ludendorf: 'If only we'd had BBC TV in the First World War!' (11 May 1982). Meanwhile, liberal opinion expressed the fear that the media was in danger of becoming the government's poodle; or, as Steve Bell put it, 'D'you wanna hear a joke, Brian? Wossa difference between a *Sun* reporter and a badly house-trained parrot?' (22 May 1982). News International and the Express Group, in particular, were in advance of the trajectory of the opinion polls in their support of government policy. There seemed to be a populist identification of mass audience with rectitude as the various discourses of national sport and history defined the terrain for debate and began to feed back into the public domain; or, as Steve Hardstaff and Rick Walker would have it, '600,000 Sheep Can't be Wrong'.

Nevertheless, government policy on the media and the reporting of the war had caused widespread dissatisfaction not only in the liberal community but also among the relatives of those in the Task Force. Gibbard's 'Sssh, from you-know-where' depicts a member of the press corps looking at the badly injured figure representing the tragically

Fig. 39   Les Gibbard, 'Ssh, from you-know-where', *The Guardian*, 14 June 1982. (By kind permission of the artist.)

successful Argentinian air attack on the troopship *Sir Galahad* at Bluff Cove. But the journalist is restrained by a military minder with John Nott in the background sporting a glass of 'Good News Fizz' (14 June 1982) (Fig. 39). W. J. Weatherby had written the day before:

> What came over clearly at the time of Vietnam was that a democracy can't function without freedom of information and speech: that politicians misuse secrecy laws intended to protect national security to cover up their mistakes, and the media are often confused about their exact role, quoting ideals of objectivity while often behaving more like a branch of government or big business or a competitor in a popularity contest.[29]

The identification of some elements of the conservative and populist press with state authority and government policy became increasingly clear as the campaign drew to a satisfactory close. Tyranny abroad became the domestic tyranny of the railway workers and the nurses. The rhetoric of the Task Force and the 'Falklands Spirit' were marshalled in the fight against the British disease and the Trade Unions (see Robert Hamilton, this volume). Waite had a bemused Task Force return to break the threatened rail strike: 'Right now, how many of you can drive trains?' (26 June 1982). While Cummings has the British people appeal to Thatcher-as-Wellington, a military and political figure, to free them from the crushing tyranny of NUPE, ASLEF and the NUR:

Fig. 40 Cummings, 'I wish our all-conquering Field Marshal could liberate the British islands from the Union Junta!', *Sunday Express*, 26 June 1982. (By kind permission of Express Newspapers plc.)

'I wish our all-conquering Field Marshal could liberate the British Islands from the Union Junta' (26 June 1982) (Fig. 40); and Franklin's British bulldog of the Task Force hoists the Union Jack as the mongrel of the NUR pees on the the flag pole (28 June 1982).[30]

Bell's strip on the day the *Belgrano* was torpedoed tackles the obfuscating domestic effect of rising war hysteria directly by drawing on the discourses of military professionalism, the Secret Mission, cold war rhetoric and government employment policies in an absurd pantomine which mirrors the conflation that had taken place in the representation of the war as Thatcher's Special Iron Lady Service and Tebbit's Special Bike Service assault a Job Centre.

With the scent of Falklands victory, success was guaranteed for the government; indeed, electoral triumphs soon followed. Gibbard illustrates the phenomenon in his eloquent 'Ground spotter to Flying Fortress! Runway out of action – but she seems to have developed vertical takeoff!' (3 May 1982). Denis Healey tries to direct operations from a foxhole on the edge of 'Tory Competence Airfield', while Michael Foot, Leader of the Labour Party, circles as a Vulcan dropping bombs, while Thatcher-as-Harrier takes off amid 'Falklands War Fever' to escape the political consequences of what had been a diplomatic débâcle and what still was economic recession, rising unemployment and increasing industrial unrest. In the liberal press, Foot in the embodiment of the Vulcan is representative of an inefficient and obsolete order that had, in fact, failed in its mission to decommission the Port Stanley airstrip. Franklin's 'The Blitz at home' (3 May 1982), on the other hand, portrays Thatcher as a Vulcan pilot putting Foot to flight in his decrepit campaign wagon, while David Steel and Roy Jenkins of the Alliance try to escape on a collapsing tandem in a delusory parallel of the raid. But this is an image in the mould of 'might is right' rather than failure and obsolescence. By the end of the conflict, the Official Opposition in the House of Commons, the Trade Union movement and the unemployed had become the enemy within: Franklin, for example, identifies Foot with all the characteristics of a military dictatorship and visualizes dissent's predicament when he says to the drunken General, 'I know your feelings, Leopoldo, no one loves me either!' (18 June 1982).

Standards of professionalism, courage, integrity and belief in cartoon are not at issue. But what are, are the unspoken premises that guide commentary. Democracy demands that the people rule, but large sectors of the press disseminate potent oversimplifications in various national narratives whose parameters are defined by the interests of individual ownership, advertising, government and, finally, the military. These stand in opposition to the interests of a significant proportion of the population who were perceived as a threat to government authority and, therefore, paradoxically, a threat to democracy. By these mechanisms dissent was controlled, reduced and driven from the arena of effective political debate.[31]

Notes

An earlier version of this essay appeared as 'Government Health Warning: Cartoons can Damage your Health', in J. Aulich and T. Wilcox (eds) (1988). *The Falklands Factor: Representations of a Conflict*, exhib. cat., Manchester, Manchester City Art Galleries.

1 See Anderson, B. (1983). *Imagined Communities: Reflections on the Origin and Spread of Nationalism*. London, Verso; Barnett, A. (1990). 'Cambodia will never disappear', *New Left Review*, Vol. 180, 101–126; Hobsbawm E. J. (1980). *Nations and Nationalism since 1870: Programme, Myth, Reality*. Cambridge, Cambridge University Press.
2 Quoted by Hiley, N. (1987). *Times Literary Supplement*, 16–22 October, p. 1149.
3 See Curran, J. and Seaton, J. (1988). *Power without Responsibility: The Press and Broadcasting in Britain*. London, Routledge; *Royal Commission on the Press 1974–7 Final Report*, Cmnd 6810, London, HMSO, 1977; House of Commons Defence Committee (1982). *The Handling of Press and Public Information During the Falklands Conflict*, Vols HC 17-I and HC 17-II; Morrison, D. and Tumber, H. (1988). *Journalists at War: The Dynamics of News Reporting During the Falklands Conflict*. London, Sage.
4 Attempts at negotiations carried out by Alexander Haig and Francis Pym began on 7 April 1982 and ended on 20 May 1982.

5 Briggs, R. (1985). *The Tin-Pot Foreign General and the Old Iron Woman*. London, Hamish Hamilton.

6 17 April 1982.

7 *La Nacion*, Buenos Aires, 28 March 1982.

8 *The Guardian*, 25 April 1982.

9 'Generals wrote in all seriousness of the English military advantages of prior training in football, and it was considered plucky and spirited to kick a football through No Man's Land on the way to an enemy trench.' See Showalter, E. (1985). *The Female Malady, Women, Madness, and English Culture, 1830–1980*. New York, Pantheon.

10 *Daily Mirror*, 21 May 1982.

11 See the *New Statesman*, 7 June 1985.

12 See *Up the Falklands! Cartoons from the Royal Marines*. Poole, Blandford Press, 1982.

13 Garland had the jackboot of the Argentine military bitten off in front of world opinion; Franklin the Union Jack hoisted (28 June 82); and Waite an unpalatable unopened tin of Argentine corned beef devoured as an ironic measure of British fortitude (5 April 82).

14 *Gentleman's Magazine* (1881). Quoted in Hugh Cunningham, 'Who speaks for Britain?', *New Society*, 22 April 1982.

15 See Surel, J., in Samuel, R. (ed). (1989). *Patriotism: The Making and Unmaking of British National Identity. Vol. III: National Fictions*. London, Routledge.

16 *A Message from the Falklands: The Life and Gallant Death of David Tinker, Lieut. RN*, compiled by Tinker, H. (1982). London, Junction Books, p. 188.

17 'South Atlantic Souvenirs' (1988). *The Falklands Factor: Representations of a Conflict*, exhib. cat., Manchester, Manchester City Art Galleries, p. 41. Two other postcard firms are worthy of note: the first, Leeds Postcards published material from a broadly similar ideological point of view as South Atlantic, while Ron Griffiths' 'King of the Mods Modern Postcards' propagated an extreme right-wing view.

18 Likewise, Gerald Scarfe's design for an exhibition poster for Bradford City Art Gallery, *The Ghosts of the Belgrano*, was judged to be too critical of the government by the leader of of the City Council and therefore too sensitive for a poster and its design was rejected. The period of the campaign also saw Steve Bell censored for reasons of good taste with 'Boom! Whamm! Thudd! Pym!' on the day *The Guardian* published pictures of *HMS Sheffield*.

19 Paulton and London, The Cresset Press, 1938.

20 Design for cover of *South*, an English language magazine dealing with Third World affairs.

21 Steve Bell works on the strip a week at a time which slightly inhibits the possibility of responding to events as they occur; but, at the same time, releases the cartoonist to take a longer view. Furthermore, *If* is published in strip form on a daily basis and this provides the reader with an unusual sense of continuity.

22 Cummings takes a swipe at Bell in 'Members of the crew! An Argentinian missile approaches! We will have an emergency debate to discuss whether we shoot it down! If Michael Foot were Admiral commanding the Task Force!' (19 May 1982).

23 A tradition put to good use by Gibbard in relation to Al Haig's political career as Reagan expostulates 'Darned fool Albatross has shot itself! Get some wings from the quartermaster and get us out of here!' (28 June 1982).

24 'The careless talk that is costing lives', *The Guardian*, 30 May 1982.

25 See Warner, M. (1985). *Monuments and Maidens: The Allegory of the Human Form*. Picador, published by Pan Books, London.

26 Dresser, M., 'Britannia', in Samuel, R., op. cit., note 15, Vol. III, pp. 26–49.

27 *New Society*, 29 April 1982.

28 The Press Council (1984). *The Press and the People 1982/3: 29th/30th Annual Report of the Press Council*. London, Press Council, pp. 147–8.

29 *The Guardian*, 13 June 1982, p. 19. Besides Bell, John Kent of the *Daily Mail*, Heath of the *Spectator*, Waite and Garland addressed the issue, while others like Cummings and Breeze of the *Daily Express* identified virtually any dissent with treason. It is interesting to note that the sales of *The Sun* fell during the conflict and over the period of 1982 the total number of daily newspaper sales fell by 600 000.

30 This tendency grew to such a pitch that Ray Buckton, general secretary of the rail union ASLEF, took out a complaint to the Press Council against an ambiguous, 'ill-conceived and vicious' cartoon by Giles featuring a poster declaring 'ASLEF – Follow Your Leader – shut the trains down NOW' with the caption 'You'd think while the forces are fighting Fascists he'd shut his trap about flexible rostering' (25 May 1982). See op. cit., note 28, p. 147.

31 See Chomsky, N. (1989). *Necessary Illusions. Thought Control in Democratic Societies*. Pluto, London.

| **6** | A Limited Engagement: Falklands Fictions and the English Novel

Nigel Leigh

Critics on both sides of the Atlantic continue to attack the contemporary English novel for its flatness, gentility, insularity and unwillingness to take imaginative chances. In his recent polemic *A Vain Conceit*, a challenging study of British fiction in the last decade, D. J. Taylor describes a situation in which, almost without exception, our major writers are guilty of a range of artistic crimes and misdemeanours, the most serious being a reluctance to engage with the task of 'defining the 1980s'.[1] Our writers seem according to Taylor, unable to write 'meaningful books about the society they inhabit'. They fail because

> they are unable to perceive, or do not wish to, the powerful forces at work in society which really influence the way we think and act: America, television, the global money marketplace, and especially language, the constantly revivifying, endlessly self-renewing language of transatlantic and transcontinental culture.

When critics say such things, they are often drawing attention to the difficulty British novelists have in finding subjects of scale from within our culture that have a distinct appeal to readers. At a time when the mainstream novel of personal relationships, working-class realism and feminist writing – the forms that have dominated our literary culture since the 1950s – are somewhat demoralized, a minority of British writers arguably do succeed in producing texts that are appropriate to our time. In *Money* (1984) and *London Fields* (1989), Martin Amis has developed a uniquely convincing transatlantic narrative voice; Salman Rushdie, under the influence of the Latin American magical realists in *Midnight's Children* (1981) and *The Satanic Verses* (1988), is now creating what can only be called a type of world literature; and Alisdair Gray, a Glaswegian James Joyce, writes narratives that provide the frisson of the real when it comes to both our inner and outer lives – *1982, Janine* (1984), *Something Leather* (1990) – as well as the grander

imaginative satisfactions of mythopoeic writing on an epic scale –
Lanark (1981). However, any list of such examples is inevitably short.

The recapture of the Falkland Islands, the most important British
foreign policy event since Suez in 1956, undoubtedly changed the
Zeitgeist in this country in the early 1980s. It created a unique spirit in
post-war Britain, one preoccupied with national unity, cultural superiority and self-determination in a way probably not experienced by any
British person under the age of 50. The two major Falklands films,
Tumbledown (1988) and *Resurrected* (1988), constructed around the
narrative device of the returning veteran, are clearly responses to this
cultural theme and have been highly successful, both with critics and
with audiences. Playwrights, too, have been quick to create theatre that
responds to our experience of the war. Ian Curteis's *Falklands Play*
(1987) was originally commissioned by the BBC, then dropped for its
hagiographic identification with the prime minister; Jeff Noon's more
critical Falklands play, *Woundings* (1986), won the Mobil Drama
Award; Steven Berkoff wrote a still under-performed poetic drama,
Sink the Belgrano (1987).

The key military conflicts of the twentieth century have undeniably
been turning points for the novel. The First World War generated a
fiction of great technical experiment, because, as Preston *et al.* have
pointed out:

> The World War of 1914–18 had a most serious effect on the
> society of the whole world. Its physical consequences alone were
> enough to slow the onward march of civilization and to destroy
> the general belief in the inevitability of human progress which had
> marked much of the philosophy of the nineteenth century.[2]

The disillusion of the intellectual class, rooted in a sense of being
displaced in a changed world, became a trademark in the literature of
the Lost Generation thrown up during the war and the early 1920s
(Hemingway, e. e. cummings, Dos Passos). The Second World War
created a completely new literary climate in Europe and the USA because it actually brought about a new order in the world, in which
realism, liberal humanism and ideology were exchanged by novelists for
a concern with experience, existentialism, cynicism and sex. It was a
war that produced its own adult bestsellers, full of unvarnished truths,
reportage and strong language. In our own time, Vietnam may have left
US writers with a legacy of guilt, anger, confusion and pessimism (a
hallmark of US novels of the late 1960s and 1970s that were not
preoccupied with technical experiment or post-modern irony), but it
also generated a great deal of compelling writing.

Thus the Falklands War would seem to offer some obvious thematic
opportunities for British novelists of all political persuasions in the
1980s, for those who want to exploit nationalism, and for those who
wish to explore what the cultural critic Anthony Barnett has called the

'pathology of British politics'.[3] The following pages examine the way British fiction writers have handled the subject of the Falklands War of 1982, and look in particular at examples of the combat novel, the thriller and the literary novel to locate a range of literary responses to the war in British writing of the 1980s.

Combat Fiction

The 1970s saw a proliferation of specialized one-author series of Second World War combat fiction. In 1976, David Williams started *Tank*; in 1978, Matthew Holden began *Squadron*, joining Frederick E. Smith's bulkier *633 Squadron* (1956) and its sequels. Although such novels have a very low literary profile and seldom get reviewed, they are very popular with publishers and are usually reprinted an amazing number of times. In the 1980s, the Falklands War inspired one long-running combat series, the *Strike Force Falklands* novels by Adam Hardy (aka Kenneth Bulmer), which consists of six books published between 1983 and 1985: *Operation Exocet, Raider's Dawn, Red Alert, Recce Patrol, Covert Op* and *'Ware Mines*.

The series follows the adventures of the Special Strike Force in the Falklands whose mission is to destroy, among other things, an enemy airfield on Stonegate Island and 'create merry hell' (*Raider's Dawn*, p. 8). As a unit, they represent military excellence:

> Anybody selected by Major Dan Granville for Strike Force had to have certain traits to have been chosen in the first place.... He had to be tough, competent in a number of military disciplines, bloody-minded, resolute, determined, motivated. He had to have a sense of humour that could handle disaster. Physical stamina was of immense importance. Mental stamina was more important (*Raider's Dawn*, p. 7).

The enemy are invariably referred to as Argies and the politics of the conflict are never in doubt:

> If only the stupid Argies hadn't been so damned greedy and tried to steal what wasn't theirs.... If only they had a decent lot in government in Argentina instead of the miserable bunch of latter-day fascist dictators.... If only Britain had told the Argies to sod off and let the Argies know she meant it (*Raider's Dawn*, p. 17).

We follow the exploits of Burnaby, Hammond, Spider, Splodge, Taff and the Whizz Kid as they *tab or yomp*[4] their way around the islands. At the end of *Raider's Dawn*, they are resolved to see the conflict through to the end: 'They had to make their way somehow to Port Stanley and chuck the Argies out of the Falklands for good' (p. 158); 'There was a long pull ahead for the Task Force before the Falklands were back where they rightfully belonged' (p. 160). The unit is tired, dishevelled and grimy, but there is no doubt that the British will pull through in the end, and national honour will be salvaged.

Although it deals with the same material as the Special Strike Force series, Walter Winward's *Rainbow Soldiers* (1985) is a more sophisticated combat fiction on a slightly higher, more mature level. In several prefatory statements, Winward is keen to remind us of his literary ambitions and reinforce his text's status as a work of invention, a created fiction: 'I have attempted to make this story as accurate as possible. However, it remains a story and whenever research and story-line have clashed, I have favoured the latter'; 'This is a work of fiction. Daddy Rankin's battalion did not exist. Its spirit did.' The structure of the book is provided by three sections that separate the narrative by time. Part One deals with the period from December 1981 to 2 April 1982, mostly in peacetime England; Part Two covers 4 April to 21 May; Part Three focuses on 21 May to 18 June. Each chapter within the three sections is headed with a character's name but the narrative voice remains in third-person.

Again the centre of dramatic attention is a group of soldiers in combat, with names like Legless Jones, Groggy Butler, Scarlett O'Hara, Three-Piece Sweet and Branston Pickles. But, unlike the *Special Strike Force* series, *Rainbow Soldiers* is anxious to develop a fiction that includes and humanizes the enemy, who are not just demonized Argies. The way Winward achieves this is to include Argentinian characters, notably Captain Ricardo Jordan-Arditti, the fiancé of an English girl, Sara Ballantine, whose brother Peter commands a company in Colonel Rankin's battalion. In the novel's melodrama, two men who had once been friends at an English school now face each other in opposing armies, friends 'separated by hemispheres' (p. 59). Winward is careful to make Arditti a sympathetic character throughout: 'Whatever he might think of the junta privately – and like many other officers of his age and rank he was anxious to see a return to democratic government – he could not allow his country's leaders to be criticized openly' (p. 50). In the conflict itself, towards the end of the novel, Arditti goes on to survive the death of both his brother, Beto, and Peter Ballantine, who catches a sniper's bullet. After the war Arditti cannot be reunited with Sara: 'Well, they met again in 1984, looked at one another a couple of times, had several drinks, then decided to fold their tents and softly steal away. It should have been different, forgive and forget. But life isn't like that' (p. 340). History, the war, has come between them forever.

Another ambitious combat novel is Alexander Fullerton's *Special Deliverance* (1987). Like the *Special Strike Force* novels, its central focus is a crack group of highly trained Special Boat Service (SBS) operatives on a near-impossible search-and-destroy mission, in this case to sabotage Argentina's stock of Exocet missiles. Yet, like *Rainbow*

Soldiers, it attempts to accommodate both sides of the conflict. The device used to achieve this is even more dramatic than Winward's star-crossed lovers and stymied friends. In Fullerton's narrative, a civilian recruited to the SBS team as an interpreter and guide, Andy MacEwen, is pitted against his brother, a commander in the Argentine Navy Air Force ('My brother won't be talking about the Falklands, he'll be calling them the Malvinas', p. 9). The Anglo-Argentine family divided by the war is a theme that requires a considerable novelistic range, and everywhere in *Special Deliverance* there are signs of extensive, though laboured, South American research. Fullerton rarely misses an opportunity to use local Spanish terms and explain them to his readers: 'She brought *chorizos*, a kind of spicy sausage, and *galletas*' (p. 54); 'There was supposed to be a *mojon* hereabouts.... A *mojon* was a stone cairn' (p. 66); '*Asado* meaning "barbecue"' (p. 47). Coupled with these dictionary definitions is a cultivation of a rudimentary understanding of 'the Latin temperament, all the macho nonsense' (p. 147). Yet the special deliverance that is experienced, punning on the trajectory of the Exocet missile, is exclusively the rite-of-passage of the English soldiers, for whom the Falklands is a positive psychological and emotional event. In the end everything is 'mere triviality in comparison with one's recent experience, the huge, extraordinary achievement' (p. 314).

The Thriller

The most distinguished adventure thriller on the Falklands is undoubtedly *Exocet* (1983), completed within a year of the conflict by Jack Higgins. Of all the pseudonyms Harry Patterson writes under, Jack Higgins is by far the best known. Although he has published prolifically as Martin Fallon (Higgins' apprenticeship as a suspense writer, featuring the special agent Paul Chavasse), Hugh Marlowe (flawed narratives with shallow characterization), James Graham (high adventure in the manner of Alistair MacLean) and Harry Patterson (*Dillinger*, 1983), it is the Higgins novels that have caught the public imagination and brought massive popularity. His breakthrough came in 1972 with the thriller *The Savage Day*, which dealt with the early years of the Irish Troubles and involved, for the first time, what Higgins now recognizes as a 'serious political theme'.[5] His classic trademark thriller *The Eagle Has Landed* (1975) refined this technique, narrating the story of a hypothetical secret Nazi operation to kidnap Winston Churchill in 1943.

The Higgins formula is to keep any underlying political, moral or religious theme contained within the structure of the thriller. In *Exocet*, Higgins creates a situation in which Russians plot to assist Argentina's effort to obtain more Exocet missiles to use against the British forces in the Falklands. We identify with the secret British intelligence agency

DI5 as it fights against all the odds to foil the hijack of the French missiles. Using the Falklands in this way not only keeps Higgins' narrative contemporary and relevant for a 1980s audience, it allows him to update the Second World War theme that had worked so well in *Eagle* and *Storm Warning* (1976). Effectively, *Exocet* represents an outgrowth of that minor tradition of British thriller novels that have traded heavily on the idea of a secret history of the War, the leading examples of this tradition being Ken Follet's *Eye of the Needle* (1979), Frederick Forsyth's *The Odessa File* (1972) and Higgins' *The Eagle Has Landed*. These books resonate with the public because they create wild, imagined scenarios that are entirely continuous with the known history. And the trick they play is to exploit an idea that already exists as a possibility in the mind of the reader, such as the presence of German agents in Scotland or an Organisation de L'Armee Secrete (OAS) assassination attempt on de Gaulle.

Placing the Russians at the centre of his narrative, Higgins is able to treat the Falklands conflict as if it were in essence yet another cold war story, an espionage narrative involving the secret services of Great Britain, the USA and the USSR and what the critic Bruce Merry calls the 'standard recurrent situations'[6] of the genre. Higgins' Soviet agent, Belov, based in Paris, links the various narrative strands together. His aim, of course, is to encourage his own ideological interests war. As he explains to his mistress:

> There is more than one reason for taking an interest in this business. A mini-war we are not involved in personally, is always useful, especially when it sets two anti-communist countries at each other's throats. A great deal of technical information can be derived from their use of weaponry and so on (p. 52).

The war is treated as if it were a massive international convenience for all parties. One of the senior British military characters points out that for both the British and the Argentinians the invasion of the Falklands might 'prove a very welcome diversion' (p. 21) from events at home. 'Bread and circuses', says another. Higgins even manages to find a heroic role for the CIA, who, always ahead of everyone else, are able to warn the British Establishment in coded messages that 'The Argentinians will hit the Falklands within the next few days' (p. 33).

Clearly, *Exocet* attempts to extend the limits of credibility and simultaneously render its plot plausible, which is the constant challenge that the thriller form takes up, but it fails to succeed where it matters, in the creation of a secret history of the Falklands that meets the expectations of the folk-mind of its audience. Finally, it has to be acknowledged that the cold war model cannot be applied universally, especially with a war which seems so post-modern in the context of late twentieth-century English history, and a conflict whose geographical tensions are so obviously North–South rather than East–West.

Also in the Higgins mould are the thrillers *Conquistadores* (1985) and *Avenge the Belgrano* (1989) by the one-time television presenter Bob Langley. In *Conquistadores*, Langley, unlike any other British writer, has a North–South perspective and goes as far as to actually set his fiction in Buenos Aires in the months before the outbreak of the Falklands War. Furthermore, his two main characters are non-English: Segunda, an Argentinian guerrilla, and David Ryker, a Texan innocent abroad. The only main English character is Magnus Stone, a millionaire and Antarctic naturalist, described as 'the only man in England who knows what's going on down there' (p. 75). As the critic Ronald Binns has pointed out, 'it has been exceptional for novelists in Britain to write fiction set in Latin America',[7] and Langley's work, along with Nicholas Shakespeare's ambitious novel of Peruvian history, *The Vision of Elena Silves* (1989), and Iain Banks's *Canal Dreams* (1989) about US skulduggery in Panama, can be seen as a sign that the region is no longer *terra incognita*. Banks's novel transcends the thriller genre and turns into what is in effect a *fin-de-siècle* novel about ecological catastrophe and social disintegration; the issue for Langley is Antarctic mineral rights and Argentina's colonial interests in the area. As Stone points out:

> If the seismograph readings prove correct, the Antarctic Peninsula could be the world's last big oil bonanza. At the moment, it's not worth touching. Getting it out under such harsh climactic conditions, transporting it back across the Cape Horn waters would be a monumental operation. But by the turn of the century, when technology will have progressed to a much more efficient level, when the industrial nations may be facing energy starvation, our entire future may depend upon what lies beneath Antarctica. The Argentines intend to grab it for themselves (p. 117).

Galtieri's new regime see themselves as the face of the future. 'We are the new *conquistadores*' (p. 237), Segunda declares, 'the Malvinas are Argentine'; and the British, as Stone observes, are a tired *ancien régime*: 'Maintaining colonies in the 1980s can be an expensive business. I've suspected for years that the British government would like to relinquish its Falklands responsibilities' (p. 241). But the Argentine character is presented as having one 'fundamental flaw, the spirit of *machismo*', which leads to its overextending itself militarily. The novel ends on a prophetic note, warning of future problems: '. . . the Falklands are the gateway to Antarctica. That's where the real issue lies. If the Argentines can remove us from these islands, they'll have opened the way for a military takeover of British Antarctic Territories when the treaty comes to an end' (p. 242). This, the book argues, is 'what this dispute is all about', locating a visionary aspect to the conflict. In the end, 1000 miles south of the Falklands, 'the source of Magnus Stone's solitary obsession, the oil and mineral wealth of the Antarctic Peninsula, still lies waiting and untouched' (p. 247). In reality, there are no human conquistadores.

Undoubtedly, the oddest novel to deal with the conflict is *The Falklands Whale* (1985) by Pierre Boulle, famous for *Bridge on the River Kwai* (1954) and *Planet of the Apes* (1973). Like *Conquistadores*, *The Falklands Whale* looks beyond the clash of ideologies and post-colonial international relations to green or ecological issues, in this case inspired by an observation of the Duke of Edinburgh's from his address to the Council for Environmental Conservation in May 1982: 'Unfortunately, whales return an echo on radar screens which is exactly like that of a submarine. I can only assume that a great many of them have been killed as a result' (epigraph). In Boulle's bizarre and sentimental story, *Moby Dick* (1851) reworked by a liberal imagination, a love affair develops between a British destroyer, the *Daring*, and a blue whale wounded by savage killer orcs. In return for the protection offered by the ship, the whale assists the expeditionary force: 'For a few moments she swam alongside the ship, then forged ahead of the convoy to take up her self-appointed post as vigilant scout spearheading the armada of the fierce fighting men pledged to recapture the Falkland Islands' (p. 97). Towards the end of the novel, when war breaks out, the men sense that the whale has 'adapted to a state of war' (p. 135), using her own radar, diving for cover, 'taking refuge from man's destructive folly'. The climax of the novel is a battle between an Argentinian submarine, 'small and shopworn' (p. 163) but determined to avenge the Argentinians who have perished in the Falklands, and the *Daring*. Intercepting a torpedo, the whale sacrifices itself, and what we are left with is an image of nature regaining its power to threaten mankind: 'When the war in the Falklands ended, there was peace again in that doorway to Antarctica, domain of the seal, the penguin, and a few blue whales that came back to haunt those waters despite the recurring threat of relentless harpooners' (p. 169). The message, for Boulle, is a planetary one.

The Literary Novel

Although there are passing references to the Falklands in a number of literary novels, including *The Satanic Verses* and Graham Swift's *Out of This World* (1988), and the conflict is one of the shaping factors behind Paul Theroux's nightmare fictional scenario for the future, *The O-Zone* (1985), there is only one mainstream state-of-the-nation novel that puts the war in any perspective. *Swansong* (1986) by Richard Francis depicts an early 1980s Britain in seedy decline, sinking under the weight of an overbearing prime minister, Mrs Kathleen Cheeseman, a grocer's daughter whose only sister runs a fruit and vegetable stall in Battersea because the family business was sacrificed for Kath's education. As a cover for the discovery that her monetarist policies are only Keynesianism in drag, she engineers a winnable war in the South Atlantic, a 'small war' to bring about an economic sea-change and social renewal.

Francis, an undeservedly neglected writer, published four highly individual novels between 1979 and 1986: *Blackpool Vanishes*, *Daggerman* (both described as novels with poems), *The Enormous Dwarf* and *The Whispering Gallery*. Each of them, according to Francis, focuses on the same central issue, 'an attempt to reveal the implications of an alien perspective in the "normal" world, in effect to explore the possibilities of transcendentalism'.[8] In *Blackpool Vanishes*, this perspective is provided by 'interterrestrial life', beings not from other worlds but from 'interstices in what we complacently think of as the continuum of reality'. In *Daggerman*, this alien vision belongs to the deranged consciousness of a Ripper-style mass-murderer. *The Enormous Dwarf* wrestles with the problem of accommodating in the present a past event so horrific that it challenges reconstruction.

In the two most recent novels, this theme has modulated into an examination of the effectiveness of 'human accounts of reality'. In *The Whispering Gallery*, the account in question is that presented by the news. In the Falklands novel, *Swansong*, the account is politics, what Francis calls 'strategies for changing the world'. One of the most intriguing such strategies for Francis is monetarism, the fashionable economic ethic of early 1980s Britain. Mrs Cheeseman's senior political adviser on the economy, Joseph Harper, is shown to be a monetarist on the verge of losing his faith, plagued with ineffable doubts: '. . . it was something other, something he couldn't quite put his finger on, a certain intangible something that merely seemed to flit around the identifiable problems, brushing against them in passing' (p. 96). His mind is making an atavistic return to Keynesianism. But as Harper's worldview crumbles, he comes to realize that Mrs Cheeseman is leading Britain inevitably to war over a small, unimportant piece of territory. Another intellectual adviser, tougher-minded than Harper, and whose star is rising, is Raymond Durrant, a transactional analyst, the minister responsible for military strategy and a proponent of 'milking the grid' (p. 154): 'Power was on tap everywhere: in that sense the grid was like one of the electrical variety. At any given juxtaposition between people, a power game was played out, and social energy was correspondingly being made available' (p. 155). We are in the realm of fantasies made social, dreams made into policies.

However, the very image of the historical present is constantly undercut by interventions from and revelations of the past. A dominant local family from the part of Shropshire in which much of the novel is set is found by a village historian to have played a role in the colonial history of the bleak South Atlantic Farquhar Island: 'Thomas took a commission to sail to Farquhar Island in the farthest corner of the South Atlantic, where a fort was built, and any Spanish or French settlers were to be persuaded to leave. He had never returned, much to his chronicler's satisfaction, and nothing was known about his fate' (p. 30). And Mrs Cheeseman's own past, particularly the banal austerity of her cornershop childhood in the 1930s, is transmuted into a political philosophy, something to be valued: 'School smelled of wee and steadily moved towards incomprehensibility, except for playground games which were sharp and detailed. In the 1930s your clothes prickled and people's faces were grey, although vegetables had brighter colours and when you opened a tin of corned beef its scent filled the room' (p. 145).

All the major characters in Francis's inventive group portrait find themselves in tragicomic situations. A punk rocker whose art is 'singing pig' (p. 38), Premo Bulge, joins the army because he can't do anything else and is sent off to war; a self-pitying vicar, David, leaves England to become a minister on Farquhar Island; a failed insurance agent, Terry, becomes a hero by accident in an absurd conflict over the island with the South American Costanaguans – a reference to Joseph Conrad's *Nostromo* (1904); a country squire, Frankie, is revealed as biologically a woman, who describes herself as a male homosexual trapped in a woman's body. The vast, apparently disparate cast of bizarre characters is shown as the novel progresses to be in fact subtly connected, and many of them are brought together by the Farquhar war. In the middle of the novel, the reader realizes the narrative tide is pulling all elements irresistably towards a military engagement in the South Atlantic. Although Francis's writing is comically energetic, there is an eschatological undertow in the final pages of the novel, entitled 'Songs for Yomping'. Clearly, the swansong is Britain's (although, as one US reviewer noted, the novel 'sounds warning notes for America as well'[9]), yet beyond the book's more obvious satirical points about what the critic Deboragh Moggach calls Francis's 'surreal, through-the-looking-glass England',[10] there is a reaching out in the desolate Farquhar landscape to a more generalized decline in many levels of our shared, communal reality. In the words of Premo Bulge's song, we are all in 'Shit's Creek' (p. 128).

As we can now see, with few examples to the contrary, the Falklands War has not, so far, permeated the consciousness of Britain's most prominent writers. Its main influence has been on exploitation literature and, to a lesser degree, the popular novel, where its handling has been, almost without exception, trivial, incidental and stereotyped. There has been a notable absence of novels that are slightly modified autobiographies (very common in Vietnam literature) or returning veteran fictions (which contrasts with the Falklands films *Tumbledown* and *Resurrected*, both of which are biographical – true stories – on the theme of the returning veteran). There have been remarkably few attempts among British writers at what Walter Holbling calls, in the context of Vietnam literature, 'literary sense-making',[11] and the Falklands novels discussed here are in no way an attempt to 'understand a specific historical situation'. Even *Swansong* finally retreats from the subject. 'It ends with the Falklands', says Richard Francis, 'but it isn't a war story either; I'd say it was more experimental and stylistically expanded.'[12]

Quite simply, the Falklands has not been what the Second World War was for British literature in the 1940s and 1950s (in the critic Walter Allen's words, an 'ineluctable shadow under which characters and events have their being'[13]); neither has the war been, like Vietnam for the USA in the 1960s and 1970s, an experience shared by all parts of the culture. Unlike the two World Wars and Vietnam, the Falklands has had only a limited effect on British writers and their literature. Consequently, many of the books mentioned in this essay are without a narrative image that corresponds to the known and ascertainable facts about the historical situation. And without mimesis they are not much more than what Bruce Merry calls 'readable evasions'.[14]

Clearly, there is no such phenomenon as the Falklands Novel, and it is unlikely that any such genre should emerge, although this is not to say that we will not see in the next 20 years or so the emergence of a Falklands equivalent to *The Red Badge of Courage* (1893), or *The Naked and the Dead* (1948), or even *Gravity's Rainbow* (1973). Stephen Crane wasn't born until 6 years after the end of the American Civil War; Thomas Pynchon was a baby during the Second World War he manages to recreate in such convincing detail. Mailer may have completed his war book within 3 years of the end of the Second World War, but Vonnegut waited nearly 25 years to publish his embroidered, semi-autobiographical *Slaughterhouse-Five* (1969). In the context of the widely acknowledged failure of the English novel in the last decade, it ought not to be surprising that there is so little Falklands literature. Yet it is difficult not to agree with D. J. Taylor when he insists:

> To rest supine in the wide, comforting darkness is an agreeable position, but it is not something you can do in the late 1980s. Mrs Thatcher. The European single market. The Bomb. Fundamentalist Islam. Whatever one may feel about them, they are not something you can ignore, not any more, and the writer who does so is simply not a functioning part of the world. It is time to step outside ... out on to bare, level plains of warring armies and mighty clangour from which art retreated so long ago.[15]

For the moment, the lacuna continues to speak louder than words.

Notes

1 Taylor, D. J. (1989). *A Vain Conceit*. London, Bloomsbury, p. 16.
2 Preston, Wise and Werner (1956). *Men at Arms*. New York, Doubleday, p. 273.
3 Barnett, A. (1982). 'Iron Britannia', *New Left Review*, No. 134, p. 32. This number is devoted exclusively to Barnett's extended essay.

4 For a discussion of these terms, see Beevor, A. (1990). *Inside the British Army*. London, Chatto and Windus, pp. 380–81. Beevor points out that 'yomp' is exclusively marine slang, meaning 'a heavy slog with kit across country'; 'tab' is the army version.

5 Smith, J. A. (ed.) (1983). *Crime and Mystery Writers*. London, Macmillan, p. 87.

6 Merry, B. (1977). *Anatomy of the Spy Thriller*. Dublin, Gill and Macmillan, p. 1.

7 Binns, R. (1990). 'A land on the edge of fantasy', *Times Higher Education Supplement*, 17 August, p. 12.

8 Locher, F. C. (ed.) (1981). *Contemporary Authors*, Vol. 102. Detroit, Gale Research Co., p. 193.

9 *Publisher's Weekly*, 22 September 1986, p. 22.

10 Moggach, D. (1986). 'In and out of love', *Sunday Times*, 10 August.

11 Holbling, W. (1989). 'Literary sense-making: American Vietnam fiction'. In J. Walsh and J. Aulich (eds) (1989). *Vietnam Images: War and Representation*. London, Macmillan, pp. 123–40.

12 Interview in *City Life Magazine*, Manchester, 6 June 1985, p. 9.

13 Allen, W. (1964). *Tradition and Dream*. Harmondsworth, Penguin, p. 205.

14 Op. cit., note 6, p. 5.

15 Op. cit., note 1, p. 132.

| **7** | 'When the Seas are Empty, so are the Words': Representations of the Task Force

Robert Hamilton

> And so today, we can rejoice at our success in the Falklands and take pride in the achievement of the men and women of our Task Force.
>   . . . Britain found herself again in the South Atlantic and will not look back from the victory she has won (Margaret Thatcher, 3 July 1982).

In popular memory the story of the Task Force usually conforms to a simple narrative (as indicated by John Taylor in his essay 'Touched with Glory'). It goes: Argentina invades Falkland Islands; British Government despatches Task Force; Task Force defeats Argentinians; Task Force sails home victorious and Britain is once again 'great'. Certainly, this is how the Prime Minister portrayed the events of April, May and June 1982 to a Conservative rally at the Cheltenham Race Course on 3 July. If political victory was to be secured from the 'achievement . . . of our Task Force', the narrative would have to be kept simple for propaganda purposes. All doubt concerning the despatch of the Task Force and its conduct during the Falklands conflict had to be dispelled, so that the myth of a rediscovered British identity could be sustained and the Conservative Party be acclaimed as its true guardian. In this chapter, I want to examine the Task Force across a broad field of representation in order to explore the various levels of meaning at which it functioned. It is not my intention to reiterate the details of the military victory but rather to concentrate on the discourses of the Fleet as it sailed south towards war and, to a lesser extent, on its return. In this, I want to examine the discourse of uncertainty that pervaded the decisions, events and reportage of April 1982 and its absence on the return of the Task Force.

The first mention of the possibility of a Task Force began with Mr

Constantino Davidoff's scrap metal merchants of Christian Salvesen Co., landing unannounced on South Georgia courtesy the Argentine Navy. Here they raised the Argentine flag and there followed increased tension between Britain and Argentina over the long disputed sovereignty of the Falklands. On 1 April, *The Guardian* reported that as a result of the landings Britain was sending a destroyer to the Falklands. The paper stated:

> Few doubts remained last night that the Royal Navy is preparing for a show of strength in the Falkland Islands dispute with Argentina. It was learned in Westminster that a hunter-killer submarine is already in the area and the destroyer *Exeter* has been ordered to leave Caribbean waters for the Falklands. Other preparations are said unofficially to include a small squadron of surface warships which will be ready to leave Britain in 48 hours.

The Guardian indicated that the sending of *HMS Exeter* was intended to be a diplomatic message, not 'to be misinterpreted' by the Argentine Government. In other words, it was a threat. However, the paper hinted that if it was meant to be so, it was not taken seriously in Buenos Aires. It further stated that Argentina '. . . would be glad to draw Britain into a naval commitment which the Royal Navy can hardly sustain across 7,000 miles of ocean'.

By this time, the decision to invade the Falklands had already been taken in Buenos Aires and the Argentinian invasion fleet was on its way.[1] It was the failure of such diplomatic signals that led to the invasion and later to the resignation of Britain's Foreign Secretary, Lord Carrington (along with Foreign Office ministers Humphrey Atkins and Richard Luce, leading to the decline of the influence of the Foreign Office during the crisis and the ascendancy of the Ministry of Defence). More importantly, the notion of a Task Force had been placed firmly in the political and public domain as a possible course of action, even if when first mooted it had been somewhat half-hearted.

With the Falkland Islands under Argentinian control by 2 April, the discussion of the possibility of a substantial and meaningful Task Force began in earnest in the press on 3 April. However, such a strategy was fraught with difficulty and uncertainty. The confusion of the British Government further compounded the hesitancy of the decision to use military force because as some newspapers reported the Falklands were 'almost certainly beyond military recovery'.[2] The Defence Secretary, John Nott, announced that although a new Task Force was being assembled, no decision on whether to despatch it would be made for several days. The *Daily Mirror* reported that 'Britain was on its way to war last night' and that '. . . 40 Royal Navy ships, including 2 aircraft carriers, were being made ready . . .'. But in a 'Mirror Comment' on page 2, the paper urged caution:

The Argentine action is outrageous. But this is still a dispute for diplomats and politicians to solve, not generals and admirals . . .

. . . But talk about sending 'nuclear' submarines into battle in the South Atlantic raised the temperature and the stakes. And it probably gave Argentina's military government the opportunity it was looking for.

The time to talk tough was when the Royal Navy reached the Falklands. When the seas are empty, so are the words.

Diplomacy was to be the answer and talk of Task Forces only upped the ante, such threats would only be meaningful when the Task Force was in place off the Islands. Empty seas, empty words. (*The Guardian* had reported before the invasion that the Islanders feared such talk would induce the Argentinians into more dramatic action.)

There are two points of uncertainly I should like to stress here. First, that the despatch of a Task Force would be harmful to a diplomatic solution of the dispute and to international support for the British position. Secondly, that doubt existed as to whether the Royal Navy had the means to retake the Falklands successfully. For example, a US Navy official was quoted in the *Daily Express* (5 April 1982) as saying the Royal Navy had little chance of victory. He continued: 'Britain is caught flat-footed, it has constructed a Navy for war in the NATO theatre and no longer has the ability to defend the inner ramparts of the Commonwealth.'

Such a view was reinforced by John Nott's Defence Review of 1981 in which the traditional Navy role was to be cut in favour of expanding its Polaris capability. The recommended cuts included the scrapping of HMS *Hermes*, the selling of HMS *Invincible* to the Australian Navy and the closing of the Portsmouth, Chatham and Gibraltar dockyards. The tenure of the Royal Marines was also at risk.[3] However, the First Lord of the Admiralty, Admiral Sir Henry Leach, saw the crisis as a chance for the Navy to prove itself invaluable for the defence of the realm. With foresight and planning, Leach was able to demonstrate to the War Cabinet that the Navy was capable of preparing a large and potentially successful Task Force.[4] John Nott admitted later that '. . . the Falkland Islands event proved that the [1981] defence review was mistaken' and that the crisis had provided Leach and the Royal Navy with an opportunity to . . . show that the Royal Navy could 'do it', in its traditional way.[5]

If Nott was still hesitant about the feasibility of a Task Force, the emergency debate in the House of Commons on Saturday 3 April certainly forced his hand,[6] and on 4 April he announced, '. . . Britain is preparing for war with Argentina . . .'. He added that while a diplomatic solution would be actively and intensively sought, the government would have no hesitation in giving the order to fight.

Karl Marx, in one of his most memorable passages (overquoted but appropriate here), stated 'the tradition of dead generations weighs like a nightmare on the minds of the living'.[7] There was one particular historical nightmare weighing on the minds of the politicians and the press – the Suez Crisis of 1956. In an article in the *Daily Express*, Lord George-Brown elucidated the fear:

> For the second time in a quarter of a century they [the Conservatives] made such a cock-up of affairs that they have made us the laughing stock of the world. The previous time was when Eden, Selwyn Lloyd and Anthony Head set out to topple Nasser and capture Suez. They made such a mess of it that our forces didn't arrive on time. Nasser blocked the canal and we had ignominiously to withdraw even before our Commander got ashore.[8]

The consternation caused by the shadow of Suez operated on three levels: first, cast in his role as the Nasser of South America, President Galtieri had already humiliated Britain on the international stage; secondly, if the Task Force failed to retake the Falklands, Britain would no longer be a 'player' on that stage (this fear was further compounded by the hiatus between the embarkation and arrival of the fleet which would give the Argentinian forces time to prepare a sturdy if not unbreachable defence of the Islands); thirdly, and perhaps the greatest fear, was the position the USA would adopt. Britain's failure to resolve the Suez crisis was in part due to the withdrawal of US support. Although Britain had gained international support in the United Nations through the passing of UN Resolution 502, which called for the unconditional withdrawal of Argentine forces and evoked Article 51 of the UN code to allow her to claim the right of self-defence in the protection of sovereign territory, US support was still not fully guaranteed. The State Department, seeing both Britain and Argentina as allies, wavered between the 'Latinists' and the 'Europeanists'. Alexander Haig, the US Secretary of State, was chosen to mediate between the warring parties and as a committed 'Europeanist' finally came down on the British side.[9] Winston Churchill, MP, attempted to lay the Suez ghost to rest: for Churchill, it was easy, forget the events of 1956 and remember 1967: 'Just as Nasser received his comeuppance at the hands of the Israeli's in 1967 . . . so too has General Galtieri made, what events are likely to prove, the most catastrophic blunder of his career.'[10]

General Galtieri, just like Nasser before him, would get his comeuppance. By collapsing a complex crisis into the cult of personality, Churchill was able to resolve the serious questions posed by Suez into a simple question of retribution. For the British and Argentinian governments, it was not so easy. As Michael Charlton pointed out:

> At Suez, Britain had been brought to its knees by the United States, the arbiter of the future. When Argentina invaded the Falklands, Argentine hopes and British expectations were fixed . . . on the attitudes and responses of the United States.[11]

The final outcome was shrouded in doubt. While the diplomacy continued, the Fleet (or the historically misnamed 'Armada' as it became increasingly known in the press) had to be seen to be large enough to show the junta in Buenos Aires that Britain meant business in order to apply the fullest diplomatic leverage. Furthermore, it was the Navy's chance to prove their worth and to erase the memory of Suez. To appropriate the terms of Chaos Theory, the only certainly was the uncertainty.

As the Task Force prepared to sail on 5 April, the discourse and symbolic function of the Fleet focused upon Portsmouth and in particular the carriers *HMS Hermes* and *HMS Invincible*. I have tried to show that, as far as the notion of a Task Force remained 'on paper', it operated on several levels in political, diplomatic and military spheres. As it began to take shape in reality, the nature of its representation also began to shift. Two specific features began to emerge. The first is what might be termed the gendering of the Fleet, as Anthony Barnett has pointed out: that is the marking out of the Task Force as specifically masculine. On 5 and 6 April, the press ran stories of hasty marriages (*The Sun*: 'Navy Pilot weds then goes off to war'), to photographs of wives and loved ones on the shore, and men loading beer into *HMS Hermes*. The *Daily Express* (6 April 1982) ran a story under the headline 'A Wren Waves Goodbye and Good Luck as the Fleet Sails Out', accompanied by a photograph of the Wren waving to *Hermes*. The next continued: 'The Hermes ups anchor and heads for the Falklands – with the hopes and hearts of all the girls left behind.' It is the last phrase 'all the girls left behind' that maps out the old familiar tale of men going off to war and the women who worriedly wait at home. Whatever the statistical reality of the situation (yes, it is men who generally go to war, although there are exceptions, like the Red Army and the North Vietnamese Army, for example), the filter of representation constructs the narrative of the Task Force as a masculine rite-of-passage, a ritual to be endured before achieving 'true' manhood. *The Sun* (16 April 1982) made the relationship less ambiguous. Next to a typical Page Three photograph of a topless woman wearing a pair of briefs with the word 'Invincible' inscribed on them ('Delightful Debbie Bouyland ... in the battle colours of HMS Invincible'), *The Sun* declared 'Knickers to Argentina'. The story continued:

> Britain's secret weapon in the Falklands dispute was revealed last night ... it's undie-cover warfare. Thousands of women with loved ones aboard the Navy's Task Force are sending the defiant message: Knickers to Argentina.
>
> They are sporting specially-made underwear embroidered across the front with the proud name of the ship in which a husband or boyfriend is serving.

What appears to be a minor and frivolous story emphasizes the masculinity of the Task Force. Furthermore, the sexual connotations contained therein implicitly deliver the promise of sexual indulgence on return from the South Atlantic. As the Task Force sailed it became a man's story (see John Taylor, this volume).

The second feature to emerge operated on the level of visual representation and provided what was to be a large collection of ships with a single signifier for the Task Force that was utilized by photographers, cartoonists and the strikers of commemorative medals alike. Many of the papers printed photographs of the front end of *HMS Hermes* as she edged out of the harbour. The striking visual feature of *Hermes* was its 'ski-jump' runway that provided outgoing aircraft with extra lift on take-off. It was this 'ski-jump' structure that came to stand for the Task Force in various forms of visual representation. Two notable examples were cartoons by Garland of the *Daily Telegraph* (21 May 1982) (Fig. 29) and Franklin of *The Sun* (4 May 1982). Garland's drawing portrayed Margaret Thatcher in a sailor's uniform sweeping peace proposals off the deck of *Hermes*; however, it was the 'ski-jump' that correctly identified it as the Falklands Fleet. The Franklin cartoon referred to Tony Benn's call for the return of the Task Force; pictured as a chicken with his ubiquitous pipe flying above ships cowardly dropping rotten eggs on the 'good name' of the Fleet. The significant signifier to identify the Task Force for *The Sun*'s readers was the 'ski-jump' of *Hermes*. The 'ski-jump' was significantly striking to mark out *Hermes* (a through-carrier as opposed to an aircraft carrier) as the ship that could, at a single instant, stand in for the whole Task Force and place it firmly within the framework of the Falklands. The 'ski-jump' literally denoted 'Falklands Task Force'. Apart from the historical references to the Armada and to Nelson (the *Daily Express* on 5 April 1982 mixed them to deliver the startling sub-headline: 'Our Armada Prepares in the Shadow of Nelson's Victory') and the combination of shore-side tears and jingoism, I would argue that the two key features of the departing Fleet were its secured masculinity and the symbolism of the 'ski-jump' that marked its sameness with other naval adventures but also its difference. (For further discussion of historical emblems, see James Aulich and Tim Wilcox, this volume).

It was estimated that the Task Force would take between 2 and 3 weeks to reach the Falklands. During this period, the reporting of the Fleet moved into a new phase. The journalists and photographers sailing with the Fleet had to operate within military, institutional and technical constraints. The press had to function within the military need for secrecy and not to give out information that would be of use to the enemy. *The Guardian* (6 April 1982) reported:

> The movements of the Royal Navy Task Force will be kept secret by the Ministry of Defence until it arrives in the South Atlantic in two or three weeks time. Although television pictures of *HMS*

Invincible steaming purposefully out of Portsmouth harbour may be useful as a political signal to the Argentinians, the Commanders who have to establish a blockade round the Falklands or land a military force will want to give as little information as possible about their dispositions, their strengths or their weaknesses.

The stories from the Fleet would therefore have to comply to that strategic need. All copy had to be passed through the assigned Ministry of Defence information officer (or 'Minder') and often the Captain of the ship on which the journalists were travelling. The relationship between the three could often be strained or on occasion openly hostile.[12] Copy also had to go through the Ministry of Defence in London before being released to the various agencies. Journalists were also limited to the number and length of despatches that could be sent because of the communications systems which were under pressure due to the weight of military and official signals sent between London and the Fleet each day. The limited stories and even fewer photographs revolved mainly around the preparations for war being made on board ships together with images of relaxation. On 19 April, the *Daily Mirror* printed a story of 'HMS Hermes ... at work and play'. Two photographs accompanied the story, one showing men sunbathing with the caption 'At Ease ... a welcome spell of sunshine and relaxation for the men of the flagship' juxtaposed with a photograph of men 'On Alert ... for a practice drill'. However, as peace negotiations were rejected by one side or the other, the likelihood of war seemed ever closer and the reports of relaxing soldiers began to disappear. They were increasingly replaced by stories of the state of war-readiness of the Task Force. On the following day, 20 April, the *Daily Mirror* declared on Page 1 that 'Peace Hopes Crash' and ran a story on Page 3, under the headline 'The Sniper', about a Corporal Phillips camouflaged in rags: 'The 22 year old paratrooper stands out like a sore thumb during this "dress rehearsal" on Falklands-bound *Canberra*. But on land he becomes the unseen killer, lethal at up to half-a-mile.'

What one can draw out from this is the combination of the notion of a 'dress rehearsal' with all the theatrical connotations of what was to follow, and the unseen killer on land. It is as if the play-acting is all but over and the killing is about to begin. A more dramatic example of the idea of the dawn of war was the widely distributed photograph by Press Association photographer, Martin Cleaver, of daybreak on *HMS Hermes*. Along with the Cleaver photograph, the *Daily Express* (21 April 1982) reported:

This is how our troops are preparing for war. It is dawn in the South Atlantic and already the Royal Marines are hard at work on board the carrier *Hermes*. Men on deck are silhouetted by the early light while below in a vast floodlit hanger — looking almost like a theatre stage – lies part of the fearful arsenal poised to hit the Argentinians.

Harrier jump jets are packed tightly against Sea King helicopters. And everywhere, men are ready for combat.

Again, there is the combination of theatricality, threat and the dramatic dawn. Just as the Task Force was readying itself for combat, so too did the British public have to be prepared in firm and confident terms for war.

Despite the increasing toughness of the language, one or two unflattering stories did appear concerning an 'Armada Pay Storm'. There were reported rumblings of discontent among the servicemen concerning the Local Overseas Allowance which had been fixed at £1 per day instead of an expected £4. The Ministry of Defence were investigating the claim and a spokesman reassured the press that 'the Task Force is still on time and on course'.[13] A second story appeared about the threatened Navy cuts. It was announced that the Prime Minister was considering a reprieve in the light of the crisis. However, John Nott later stated that no such reprieve was being considered. He dismissed claims that 'Navy cuts would preclude any chances of mounting a similar Task Force in the future';[14] at such a late date, the Navy had little chance of counter-argument, it had simply to perform the task at hand. On the same day, 28 April, the *Daily Express* reported what it thought to be the last despatch from Admiral Woodward, the Task Force Commander, on the eve of a total news blackout before the Fleet entered the battle zone. The story stated:

> The last words from the Task Force, before the news blackout, came from the Commander, Admiral Sandy Woodward.
> He said: 'My battle group is ready to strike. This is the run-up to the big match which should be a walkover'.

On 29 April, the *Daily Express* carried another 'last despatch' from Woodward which openly contradicted the previous one. He is reported to have said:

> ... provided there was no sudden political change from one side to the other, it could be a long war ... It's one we can do. But it's one we would much rather not do for all the good reasons that nobody wants a long and bloody campaign.

Woodward subsequently denied much of the bulk of the first despatch,[15] but the second earned him the displeasure of the Prime Minister. On 30 April, the same paper reported:

> ... Admiral Sandy Woodward has been told to keep quiet about the imminent battle in the Falklands.
> The Prime Minister herself was said to be dismayed by his latest remarks that the Task Force could be facing 'a long and bloody campaign'.

It is clear that up until the final news blackout and the beginning of hostilities with the sinking of the *General Belgrano* on 3 May that the discourse of uncertainty remained despite the efforts of the government to play down any doubts. The reports coming from the Task Force were hampered by the military need for secrecy, the admitted difficulty of the journalists to maintain an objective position while travelling with the Fleet,[16] and the institutional filter of the Ministry of Defence. But a space for questioning, if not open dissent, was still available. Woodward's remarks were perhaps made in the atmosphere of a commander facing not the possibility of casualties but the reality. As he said: 'I am not in any doubt that unless people say "let's stop" it will be a long and bloody campaign. And in my mind, it is absolutely fundamental to try and avoid it.'[17] By 4 May, it was too late. *HMS Sheffield* was sunk by a single Exocet with the loss of 30 men, in a revenge attack for the sinking of the *Belgrano*. The Falklands conflict had begun in earnest.

In the aftermath of victory, the Task Force returned in piecemeal fashion. From mid-June to mid-July, various ships carrying troops returned to be greeted euphorically as home-coming heroes, but it often had to compete for the front page with other important news stories such as the birth of Princess Diana's first baby, and the murderous escapades of Barry Pruedom.[18] There are two points I wish to draw out from the discourse of disembarkation. The first was the resolution of the Fleet's rite-of-passage. On 12 June, *The Sun* carried two stories on the return of the QE2. On Page 1, a woman was photographed baring her breasts accompanied by the headline 'Lovely to See You'. The headline was obviously meant to refer to the returning of the servicemen, but it also referred to the sight in reverse, that is the pleasure gained by the servicemen from seeing the 'Southampton Beauty'. The sexual innuendo of return was further compounded by a Page 3 report of the 'Sexy Capers on the Ocean Rave' concerning the various on-board romances of some of the 22 stewardesses who sailed with the QE2. It can be inferred that these stories represent the closure of the gendering of the Task Force as it departed in April. As in Delacroix's *Liberty Leading the People* (1830), the breast has often been represented as both promise of and reward for heroic deeds. With the Task Force returning, the reports of women baring their breasts acted as symbols of reward. It has been seen that the Fleet on embarkation was defined as a masculine rite-of-passage. On return, the passage had been completed and the reward offered, effectively closing the narrative. By 12 July, the *Daily Mirror* implied that this form of welcome had almost become traditional. On the return of the *SS Canberra* it reported:

> And for those still waiting to disembark there was a ritual form of welcome from the Erika Roe's [the Twickenham Streaker] dotted among the crowds.
>
> 'Cor' muttered a marine, as one well-shaped girl popped up

topless from behind a big flag, 'Now that's what I call a fine pair of welcomes'.

The implied reward of combat was sexual, as a banner onboard *Canberra* declared: 'Lock up your daughters! The Bootnecks are back!'[19]

Another banner on *Canberra* pointed to the second theme of the return of the Task Force; it went 'Call Off the Rail Strike ... or We'll Call an Air Strike'. The escalating rail strike of 1982 became intertwined with the end of the Falklands conflict. For example, a Keith Waite cartoon in the *Daily Mirror* showed newly arrived troops from the war being asked by their Sergeant 'Right now, how many of you can drive trains?' This combination formed part of what can be defined as the new spirit of the Task Force. It was to be applied to the solving of Britain's internal problems, the most immediate being the rail strike. In order to preserve the born-again post-Falkland's nationalism, Thatcher at the Cheltenham rally stated that:

> ... the battle of the South Atlantic was not won by ignoring the dangers or denying the risks.
>
> It was achieved by men and women who had no illusions about the difficulties. They faced them squarely and were determined to overcome. That is increasingly the mood of Britain. And that's why the rail strike won't do.[20]

The discourse of doubt and uncertainty, of the 'waverers and fainthearts', that underpinned the representation of the Task Force before and as it sailed south had been 'defeated' and now had to be extinguished at the national level (see James Aulich, this volume). The lesson was not lost on 129 civilian crewmen from *Canberra* who were informed on their return from the Falklands that they were to be made redundant.[21] They learnt to their cost that 'when the seas are empty, so are the words'.

In conclusion, I would argue that the meanings of the Task Force were complex and multiplicit. It operated on political, diplomatic, military and symbolic levels and could not be fixed to any singular or coherent narrative. It traded in sexual metaphors, was haunted by historical ghosts and acting tough, it was a bargaining chip. In the summer of 1990 another 'Task Force' in the Gulf traded in the same currency. As the crisis in the Middle East unfolded, the newspapers returned to the dockyard to report, and in some sense, re-enact the departure of warships and its attendant discourses. It would seem that the departure of the Falklands Task Force has provided the media with the post-cold war language of conflict. On 14 August 1990, the *Daily Mail* pictured 'The Sad Faces of Farewell' as it reported on the 'hopes and fears of the Minehunter Task Force and the loved ones they left behind'. The familiarity and speed with which such stories were utilized has provided the first evidence that the representation of the Falklands

Task Force can be seen as constructing a paradigm for the reporting of Third World conflicts as the likelihood of war in Europe disappears. What can be said, is that it is certain that when the seas are not empty, the words are to be the same.

Notes

1 The Sunday Times Insight Team. (1982). *The Falklands War*. London, Sphere Books, pp. 81–2.
2 *The Guardian*, 3 April 1982, p. 1.
3 Hastings, M. and Jenkins, S. (1983). *The Battle for the Falklands*. London, Michael Joseph. pp. 86–7.
4 Ibid., pp. 61–8.
5 Charlton, M. (1989). *The Little Platoon: Diplomacy and the Falklands Dispute*. Oxford, Basil Blackwell, pp. 156–7.
6 See Barnett, A. (1982). *Iron Britannia: Why Parliament Waged its Falklands War*. London, Allison and Busby.
7 Marx, K. (1969). 'The Eighteenth Brumaire of Louis Bonaparte'. In *Selected Works*, Vol. 1. Moscow, Progress, p. 398.
8 Lord George-Brown (1982). 'Why no amount of hysterical talk can save the Falklands now', *Daily Express*, 5 April, p. 16.
9 For a fuller account of Haig's shuttle diplomacy, see Charlton, op. cit., note 5, pp. 158–81.
10 Churchill, W. (1982). 'If the cry is action stations', *Daily Express*, 18 April, p. 7.
11 Op. cit., note 5, p. 157.
12 For a fuller account, see Morrison, D. E. and Tumber, H. (1988). *Journalists at War*. London, Sage, pp. 131–62.
13 Ibid., p. 141.
14 *Daily Express*, 28 April 1982, p. 3.
15 Op. cit., note 3, pp. 130–31.
16 Op. cit., note 12, pp. 95–130.
17 *Daily Express*, 30 April 1982, p. 1.
18 See *Daily Mirror*, 29 June 1982, p. 1.
19 'Bootneck' is the term for a Royal Marine.
20 Margaret Thatcher's Cheltenham speech is reprinted in full in Barnett, op. cit., note 6, pp. 149–53.
21 *The Guardian*, 13 July 1982, p. 26.

Bibliography

Joanna Rose

Adams, V. (1986). *The Media and the Falklands Campaign*. Basingstoke, Macmillan.

Adams, V. (1988). *Falklands Conflict: Flashpoints S*. Hove, Wayland.

Arthur, M. (1986). *Above All Courage: First Hand Accounts From The Falklands Front Line*. London, Sphere.

Aulich, J. and Wilcox, T. (eds) (1988). *The Falklands Factor: Representations of a Conflict*, exhib. cat., Manchester, Manchester City Art Galleries.

Barker, F., Holme, P. and Ivesson, M. (1984). *Confronting the Crisis: War Politics and Culture in the Eighties*. Colchester, University of Essex.

Barnett, A. (1982). *Iron Britannia: Why Parliament Waged Its Falklands War*. London, Allison and Busby.

Beck, P. J. (1988). *The Falkland Islands as an International Problem*. London, Routledge.

Behr, E. (1981). *Anyone Here Been Raped and Speaks English*. London, Hamish Hamilton.

Belgrano Action Group (1988). *The Unnecessary War: The Belgrano Inquiry*. Nottingham, Spokesman Books.

Benn, A. W. (1982). *On the Falklands War*. Nottingham, Spokesman Books.

Bilton, M. and Kosminsky, P. (1989). *Speaking Out: Untold Stories from the Falklands War*. London, Deutsch.

Bishop, P. and Witherow, J. (1982). *The Winter War: The Falklands*. London, Quartet.

Braybrook, R. (1982). *Battle For The Falklands*, 3 Vols. London, Osprey.

Brown, C. (1982). *The Falklands Conflict*. Cornwall, Coronet.

Brown, D. (1987). *Royal Navy and the Falklands War*. London, L. Cooper.

Burden, R. (1986). *Falklands: The Air War*. London, Arms and Armour Press.

Burns, J. (1987). *The Land that Lost Its Heroes: The Falklands, the Post-War and Alfonsin*. London, Bloomsbury.

Burns, J. (1989). *Beyond the Silver River*. London, Bloomsbury.

Byers, R. B. (1986). *The Denuclearization of the Oceans*. London, Croom Helm.

Byrd, P. (ed.) (1988). *British Foreign Policy Under Thatcher*. Hemel Hempstead, P. Allan.

Callaghan, J. (1987). *Time and Chance*. Glasgow, Collins/Fontana.

Calvert, P. (1982). *Falklands Crisis: The Rights and Wrongs*. London, F. Pinter.

Calvert, P. and Calvert, S. (1989). *Argentina: Political Culture and Instability*. London, Macmillan.

Cardozo, Kirschbaum and van der Koy (1983). *Falklands: The Secret Plot*. East Moseley, Preston Editions.

Carr, J. (1984). *Another Story: Women and the Falklands War*. London, Hamish Hamilton.

Carrington, Lord (1988). *Reflections on Things Past*. Glasgow, Collins/Fontana.

Cawkell, M. (1983). *The Falkland Story 1592–1982*. Oswestry, Anthony Nelson.

Charlton, M. (1989). *The Little Platoon: Diplomacy and the Falklands Dispute*. Oxford, Basil Blackwell.

Chatham House Special Report (1982). *The Falklands Dispute: International Dimensions*. London, Royal Institute of International Affairs.

Child, J. (1985). *Geopolitics and Conflict in South America: Quarrels among Neighbours*. New York, Praeger.

Cobb, D. (1986). *The Making of a War Artist. David Cobb: The Falklands Paintings*. London, Conway Maritime Press.

Cockerell, M., Hennessey, P. and Walker, D. (1982). *Sources Close to the Prime Minister*. London, Macmillan.

Coll, A. R. and Arend, A. C. (1985). *The Falklands War: Lessons for Strategy, Diplomacy and International Law*. London, Allen and Unwin.

Cook, J. (1985). *The Price of Freedom*. London, New English Library.

Cordesman, A. H. and Wagner, A. R. (1989). *Afghan and Falklands Conflicts and Conclusions of the Study*. London, Mansell.

Cosgrove, P. (1978). *Margaret Thatcher: A Tory and Her Party*. London, Hutchinson.

Cosgrove, P. (1985). *Carrington: A Life and Policy*. London, Dent.

Crawley, E. (1984). *A House Divided: Argentina 1880–1980*. London, C. Hurst.

Critchley, M. (1982) 'Introduction'. In *Falklands Task Force Portfolio Part 2*. Liskeard, Maritime Books.

Dabat, A. and Lorenzano, L. (1984). *Argentina, the Malvinas and the End of Military Rule*. London, Verso.

Dalyell, T. (1982). *One Man's Falklands*. London, Cecil Woolf.

Dalyell, T. (1983). *Thatcher's Torpedo: The Sinking of the Belgrano*. London, Cecil Woolf.

Dalyell, T. (1987). *Misrule ... How Mrs Thatcher Has Misled Parliament from the Sinking of the Belgrano to the Wright Affair*. London, Hamish Hamilton.

Dartford, M. (ed.) (1986). *Falklands: The Aftermath*. London, Marshall Cavendish.

Destefani, L. H. (1982). *The Malvinas, the South Georgias and the South Sandwich Islands: The Conflict with Britain*. Buenos Aires, Edipress.

Dillon, G. M. (1989). *Falklands: Politics and War*. London, Macmillan.

Dobson, C., Miller, J. and Payne, R. (1982). *The Falkland Conflict*. Cornwall, Coronet Books.

English, A. and Watts, A. J. (1982). *Battle For The Falklands. Book 2: Naval Forces*. London, Osprey.

Ethell, J. and Price, A. (1982). *Air War South Atlantic*. London, Sidgwick and Jackson.

FCO (1983). *Background Brief: The Falkland Islands – Early History*. London, FCO.

FCO (1986). *Background Brief: Claims to the Falkland Islands*. London, FCO.

Fox, R. (1982). *Eye Witness Falklands: A Personal Account of the Falklands Campaign*. London, Methuen.

Fox, R. (1985). *Antarctica and the South Atlantic: Discovery, Development and Dispute*. London, BBC.

Fowler, W. (1982). *Battle For The Falklands. Book 1: Land Forces*. London, Osprey.

Freedman, L. (1988). *Britain and the Falklands War*. Oxford, Basil Blackwell.

Freedman, L. and Gamba-Stonehouse, V. (1990). *Signals of War: The Falklands Conflict of 1982*. London, Faber and Faber.

Frost, J. (1983). *2 Para Falklands: The Battalion at War*. London, Sphere.

Fursdon, E. (1988). *Falklands Aftermath: Picking up the Pieces*. London, L. Cooper.

Gamba, V. (1987). *The Falklands/Malvinas War: A Model for North–South Crisis Prevention*. London, Allen and Unwin.

Glasgow University Media Group (1985). *War and Peace News*. Milton Keynes, Open University Press.

Goebel, J. (1927). *The Struggle for the Falklands Islands*. London, Yale University Press.

Gould, D. (1984). *On the Spot: The Sinking of the Belgrano*. London, Cecil Woolf.

Gould, D. (ed.) (1988). *Report of the Assessors on the Belgrano Inquiry*. London, Cecil Woolf.

Graham-Yooll, A. (1981). *Portrait of an Exile*. London, Junction Books.

Graham-Yooll, A. (1986). *A State of Fear: Memories of Argentina's Nightmare*. London, Eland.

Gustafson, L. S. (1988). *The Sovereignty Dispute over the Falkland (Malvinas) Islands*. New York, Oxford University Press.

Haig, A. (1984). *Caveat: Realism, Reagan and Foreign Policy*. London, Weidenfeld and Nicolson.

Hall, S. (1988). *The Hard Road to Renewal: Thatcherism and the Crisis of the Left*. London, Verso.

Hanrahan, B. and Fox, R. (1982). *I Counted Them All Out and I Counted Them All Back Again*. London, BBC.

Harries-Jenkins, G. (ed.) (1983). *Armed Forces and Welfare Societies: Challenges in the 1980s. Britain, The Netherlands, Germany, Sweden and the United States*. London, Macmillan.

Harris, R. (1983). *Gotcha! The Media, The Government and the Falklands Crisis*. London, Faber and Faber.

Hastings, M. and Jenkins, S. (1983). *The Battle for the Falklands*. London, Michael Joseph.

Henderson, Sir N. (1984). *The Private Office: A Private View of Five Foreign Secretaries and of Government from the Inside*. London, Weidenfeld and Nicolson.

Henderson, Sir N. (1987). *Channels and Tunnels*. London, Weidenfeld and Nicolson.

HMSO (1977). *Report of the Committee on the Future of Broadcasting* (The Annan Report). Cmnd. 6753. London, HMSO.

HMSO (1982a). *Britain and the Falklands Crisis: A Documentary Record*. London, HMSO.

HMSO (1982b). *The Disputed Islands*. London, HMSO.

HMSO (1982c). *The Falkland Islands: The Facts*. Foreign and Commonwealth Office, London, HMSO.

HMSO (1982d). House of Commons Defence Committee First Report 1982–83 (The HCDC Report). *The Handling of the Press and Public Information During the Falklands Conflict*, Vols I and II. London, HMSO.

HMSO (1982e). *The Falklands Campaign – A Digest of Debates in the House of Commons 2 April to 15 June 1982* (K. S. Morgan, ed.). London, HMSO.

HMSO (1983a). *The Falklands Campaign: The Lessons* (Chairman Lord Franks). London, HMSO.

HMSO (1983b). *Falkland Islands Review: Report of a Committee of Privy Councillors* (The Franks Report). Cmnd. 8787. London, HMSO.

HMSO (1983c). *The Falklands Campaign: The Lessons. Presented to Parliament by the Secretary of State For Defence.* London, HMSO.

HMSO (1983d). *Report of the Study Group on Censorship* (The Beech Report). Cmnd. 9112. London, HMSO.

HMSO (1985a). *The Protection of Military Information.* Cmnd. 9499. London, HMSO.

HMSO (1985b). *Events of the Weekend of 1st and 2nd May 1982: Third Report of the Foreign Affairs Committee, Session 1984–5.* London, HMSO.

Hoffman, F. L. and Hoffman, O. M. (1983). *Sovereignty in Dispute: Falklands/Malvinas.* San Diego, Westview Press.

Honeywell, M. and Pearce, J. (1982). *Falklands/Malvinas: Whose Crisis?* London, Latin American Bureau.

Jenkins, P. (1987). *Mrs Thatcher's Revolution: The Ending of the Socialist Era.* London, Jonathan Cape.

Jolly, R. (1983). *The Red and Green Life Machine: Diary of the Falklands Field Hospital.* London, Century.

Kitson, L. (1982). *The Falklands War: A Visual Diary By The Official War Artist Linda Kitson.* London, Mitchell Beazley, in association with The Imperial War Museum.

Knightley, P. (1975). *The First Casualty: The War Correspondent as Hero and Mythmaker.* London, Quartet.

Kon, D. (1983). *Los Chicos de la Guerra: Interviews by Daniel Kon.* London, New English Library.

Ladd, J. D. (1982). *Royal Marine Commando.* London, Hamlyn Group.

Laffin, J. (1982). *Fight for the Falklands: Why and How Britain Went to War – From Invasion to Surrender.* London, Sphere.

Lawrence, J. and Lawrence, M. C. R. (1988). *When the Fighting is Over: A Personal Story of the Battle for Tumbledown Mountain and its Aftermath.* London, Bloomsbury.

Lowenthal, A. and Fitch, J. S. (eds) (1986). *Armies and Politics in Latin America.* London, Holmes and Meier.

McGowan, R. and Hands, J. (1983). *Don't Cry For Me Sergeant Major.* London, Futura.

McManners, H. (1987). *Falklands Commando.* London, Grafton.

Mercer, D., Mungham, G. and Williams, K. (1987). *The Fog of War.* London, Heinemann.

Middlebrook, M. (1982). *Task Force: The Falklands.* Harmondsworth, Penguin.

Middlebrook, M. (1989). *The Fight for the Malvinas: The Argentine Forces in the Falklands War.* London, Viking.

Moon, B. and Moon, C. (1985). *Argentina is My Country.* Hove, Wayland.

Morrison, D. E. and Tumber, H. (1988). *Journalists at War: The Dynamics of News Reporting During the Falklands Conflict*. London, Sage.

Murray, P. (1980). *Margaret Thatcher*. London, W. H. Allen.

Pearce, J. (ed.) (1982). *The Falklands Dispute: International Dimensions*.

Peralta-Ramas, M. and Waisman, C. A. (1987). *From Military Rule to Liberal Democracy in Argentina*. London, Westview Press.

Perkins, R. (1986). *Operation Paraquat: The Battle For South Georgia*. Beckington, Picton Chippenham.

Perl, R. (ed.) (1983). *The Falkland Islands Dispute in International Law and Politics: A Documentary Sourcebook*. New York, Oceana.

Perrett, B. (1982). *Weapons of the Falklands Conflict*. Poole, Blandford.

Phipps, C. (1977). *What Future for the Falklands?* London, Fabian Society.

Ponting, C. (1985). *The Right To Know: The Inside Story of the Belgrano Affair*. London, Sphere.

Preston, A. (1982). *Sea Combat off the Falklands: The Lessons That Must Be Learned*. London, Collins Willow.

Revolutionary Communist Party (1982). *Malvinas Are Argentinas*. London, Junius.

Rice, D. and Gavshon, A. (1984). *The Sinking of the Belgrano*. London, Secker and Warburg.

Riddell, P. (1989). *The Thatcher Decade: How Britain has Changed During the 1980s*. Oxford, Basil Blackwell.

Royle, T. (1989). *War Report: The War Correspondent's View of Battle from Crimea to the Falklands*. London, Grafton.

Schoultz, L. (1983). *The Populist Challenge: Argentine Electoral Behaviour in the Postwar Era*. London, University of North Carolina Press.

Smith, G. (1985). *Death of a Rose-grower: Who Killed Hilda Murrell?* London, Cecil Woolf.

Smith, G. (1989). *Battles of the Falklands War*. Shepperton, I. Allan.

Smith, J. (1984). *74 days: Islander's Diary of the Falklands Occupation*. London, Century.

Speed, K. (1983). *Sea Change: The Battle for the Falklands and the Future of Britain's Navy*.

Sunday Express Team (1982). *War in the Falklands: The Campaign in Pictures*. London, Weidenfeld and Nicolson.

Sunday Times Insight Team (1982). *The Falklands War: The Full Story*. London, Sphere.

Thomas, G. (1985). *Mr Speaker: The Memoirs of the Viscount Tonypandy*. London, Century.

Tinker, H. (1982). *A Message From the Falklands: The Life and Death of David Tinker, Lieut. RN: From His Letters and Poems*. London, Junction Books.

Tracey, M. (1983). *In the Culture of the Eye: Ten Years of Weekend World*. London, Hutchinson.

Tunstall, J. (1983). *The Media in Britain*. London, Constable.

Underwood, G. (ed.) (1983). *Our Falklands War*. Liskeard, Maritime Books.

United Nations Security Council (1982). *Minutes of Meetings 2345 (1 April 1982)–2373 (4 June 1982)*. New York.

Vaux, N. (1986). *March to the South Atlantic: 42 Commando Royal Marines on the Falklands War*. London, Buchan and Enright.

Vaux, N. (1987). *Take That Hill: Royal Marines in the Falklands War*. Oxford, Pergamon Press.

Villar, R. (1984). *Merchant Ships at War: The Falklands Experience*. London, Conway Maritime Press.

Ward, H. G. (1988). *The Falklands Factor*. London, Settle Press.

Weston, S. (1989). *Walking Tall*. London, Bloomsbury.

Williams, P. and Power, M. (1990). *Summer Soldier: The True Story of the Missing Falklands Guardsman*. London, Bloomsbury.

Winchester, S. (1983). *Prison Diary, Argentina: A Falklands Story*. London, Chatto and Windus, The Hogarth Press.

Woodward, B. (1987). *Veil: The Secret Wars of the CIA*. London, Simon and Schuster.

Woolf, J. and Moorcroft Wilson, J. (eds) (1982). *Authors Take Sides on the Falklands*. London, Cecil Woolf.

Wright, P. (1985). *On Living in an Old Country*. London, Verso.

Young, H. (1989). *One of Us: A Biography of Margaret Thatcher*. London, Macmillan.

Fiction

Branfield, J. (1987). *The Falklands Summer*. London, Gollancz.

Berkoff, S. (1987). *Sink the Belgrano and Massage*. London, Faber and Faber.

Bond, E. (1988). *Restoration: A Pastoral*. London, Methuen.

Boulle, P. (1985). *The Falklands Whale*. London, W. H. Allen.

Briggs, R. (1985). *The Tin-Pot General and the Old Iron Woman*. London, Hamish Hamilton.

Curteis, I. (1987). *The Falklands Play*. London, Hutchinson.

Francis, R. (1986). *Swansong*. London, Flamingo.

Fullerton, A. (1987). *Special Deliverance*. Harmondsworth, Penguin.

Hardy, A. (1984a). *1. Operation Exocet*. London, Futura.

Hardy, A. (1984b). *2. Raider's Dawn*. London, Futura.

Hardy, A. (1984c). *3. Red Alert*. London, Futura.

Hardy, A. (1985a). *4. Recce Patrol*. London, Futura.

Hardy, A. (1985b). *5. Covert Op*. London, Futura.

Hardy, A. (1985c). *6. 'Ware Mines*. London, Futura.

Higgins, J. (1983). *Exocet*. London, Collins.

Holmes, R. (1985). *Firing Line*. London, Jonathan Cape.

Jacks, O. (1986). *Break-Out*. London, Grafton.

Langley, B. (1985). *Conquistadors*. London, Michael Joseph.

Langley, B. (1989). *Avenge the Belgrano*. London, Sphere.

Mooney, B. and Scarfe, G. (1985). *Father Kissmass and Mother Claws*. London, Hamish Hamilton.

Noon, J. (1986). *Woundings*. Birmingham, Oberon Books.

Perry, N. (1987). *Arrivederci Millwall*. London, Faber.

Theroux, P. (1985). *The O-Zone*. London, Hamish Hamilton.

Winward, W. (1985). *Rainbow Soldiers*. London, Hamish Hamilton.

Wood, C. (1987). *Tumbledown: A Screenplay*. Harmondsworth, Penguin.

Documentary Video

BBC Video (1982). *Falklands Task Force South*. London, BBC Enterprises.

Bilton, M. and Kosminsky, P. (1987). *The Falklands War: The Untold Story*. Yorkshire TV Production.

Denti, J. (1983). *Malvinas – A Story of Betrayals*, distributed by The Other Cinema, London.

Hands, J. (Producer). (1987). *The Commando's Tale: Falklands '82*. ITN Granada Television International.

Lewis, M. (Producer) (1982). *Battle for the Falklands*. ITN Granada Television International.

Discography

Sean Brady (1982). *The Thatcher Song*.

John Cale (1989). *The Falklands Suite*.

Elvis Costello (1983). *Shipbuilding*.

Elvis Costello (1989). *Tramp the Dirt Down*.

Crass (1982a). *Sheep Farming in the Falklands*.

Crass (1982b). *How Does it Feel (To be the Mother of a Thousand Dead)*.

Crass (1983). *Gotcha!*

Dub Syndicate (1988). *No Alternative (But to Fight)*.

The Exploited (1983). *Let's Start a War (Said Maggie one Day)*.

The Imposter (1984). *Peace in Our Time*.

Madness (1982). *Blue Skinned Beast*.

Owen Jones (1988). *Margaret's Sinking*.

Renaud (1985). *Madame Thatcher*.

Vera Lynn (1982). *I Love this Land*.

Index

Alfonsin, Raul, 2, 52
Allen, Martin, 43–4, 48
Amis, Martin, 117
Antelope, HMS, 57, (fig. 11) 68, 69, 73
Archer, Peter, (fig. 17) 77
Ardent, HMS, (fig. 19) 79–81
Argentine National Commission on
    Disappeared People, 50
Argie (film), 47–8
art therapy, 9, 10, (figs 19 and 20)
    78–81
Artistic Records Committee, 59–60,
    82
Ashton, Graham, 72–4
Asquith, Anthony, 36
Associated Press, 69
Atkins, Humphrey, 130
Avenge the Belgrano (novel), 123–4

Barnett, Anthony, 1, 118–19, 133
Beck, Peter, J., 8
Belgrano, General, 22, 29, 47, (fig.
    12) 69–70, 102, 105, 113, 137,
    115 n18
Bell, Steve, 10, 82, (fig. 26) 93–5, 98,
    (fig. 31) 100, 102, 107, 110, 111,
    113, 114, 115 n21, 115 n22, 116
    n29
Benn, Tony, 8, 104, 108, 134
Berkoff, Steven, 118
Blanco, Jorge, 47
Bleasdale, Alan, 37, 95
Born on the Fourth of July (film), 40
Boulle, Pierre, 124
Breeze, 116 n29
Briggs, Raymond, 10, 87
Britannia, (fig. 35) 104–5
Brookes, Peter, 100, (fig. 32) 101
Brown, Adrian, 5
Butler, Lady, 76

Cable News Network, 82
Caldwell, Bill, (fig. 22) 87, 88, 92, 98
Canberra, SS, 61, (fig. 7) 62, 65, 77,
    (fig. 18) 78, 79, 137–8
Caput Mortuum: A Commentary
    (sculpture), (fig. 14) 72
Carr, Warrant Officer Roy, 92
Carrington, Lord, 130
cartoon, 3, 6, 7, 8, 10, 53, 55, 63,
    84–115, 134
Castro, Fidel, 55
censorship, 13–15, 28–9, 50–7, 60,
    110, 134–5, 115 n18
Charlton, Michael, 10, 132
Chomsky, Noam, 110
Cleaver, Martin, 10, 15, 57, 69,
    135–6
Cobb, David, 76, 77
Cockerell, Michael, 8
Collages produced during post-
    traumatic stress disorder, (figs 19
    and 20) 79–82
Conquistadores (novel), 123–4
Constance, Diana, 69
Coventry, HMS (fig. 20) 80, 81
Coward, Noel, 34, 35, 42
Cummings, 92, (fig. 25) 93, 97, 98,
    102, 103–4, 111, (fig. 40)
    112–13, 115 n22, 116 n29
Cuneo, Terence, 77
Curteis, Ian, 38, 118

Davidoff, Constanino, 129–30
*Dawn over the South Atlantic on
    board HMS Hermes*, 100, (fig.
    33) 101, 135–6
Delors, Jacques, 92
Deluge, 74, (fig. 16) 75

Edwardes, Kit, 69
Evans, David, 65

Exeter, HMS, 130
Exocet (novel), 121–2
Eyre, Richard, 10, 39, 41, 48

Falklands Medal (montage), (fig. 11)
    68
Falklands Play (drama), 118
Falklands Task Force Crownmedal,
    70, (fig. 13) 71
Falklands: The Secret Plot, 10–11
Fascio/Fiasco (sculpture), (fig. 15)
    73–4
Faulkes, Wally, 86, 89
film, ix, 3, 9–10, 33–49
fine art, 3–4, 10, 58–83
First World War, 10, 24, 26, 74, 76,
    82, 111, 118
Foot, Michael, 8, 113–14, 115 n22
football, x, 8, 10, 47, (fig. 23) 88–93,
    110, 114 n9
For Queen and Country (film), 36,
    44–6, 48–9
Francis, Richard, 124–6
Franklin, Stanley, 8, (fig. 24) 91–2,
    97, 102, 113, 114, 134, 115 n13
Fullerton, Alexander, 120–1
Furniss, Rosalind, 65

Galahad, Sir, 26, 27
Galtieri, General Leopoldo, 1–2, 4, 7,
    47, 51, 54, (fig. 21) 86, 97, 109,
    114, 123, 132
Gardel, Carlos, 53, 55
Garland, Nicholas, 86, (fig. 34) 103,
    (fig. 35) 104–5, 109, 110, 134,
    115 n13, 116 n29
Gibbard Les, 86, 89, (fig. 29) 98, 103,
    108, 110, (figs 38 and 39)
    111–12, 113, 116 n23
Giles, Carl, (fig. 28) 93–7, 98, 116
    n30
Gorbachev, Mikhail, 37
Gough, Paul, 74
Gray, Alisdair, 117
Greenaway, Peter, x
Greengrass, Paul, 10, 34, 37, 42–6,
    48
Griffiths, Ron, 115 n17

Haig, General Alexander, (fig. 21) 86,
    132, 114 n4, 116 n23

Hardstaff, Steve, 94, 111
Hardy, Adam, 119–21
Harvey, David, 1
Hastings, Max, 65, 69
Healey, Denis, 113
Heath, Edward, 116 n29
Hermes, HMS, 99–100, (fig. 33) 101,
    131, 133–6
Higgins, Jack, 121–2
Hopkins, David, (figs 36 and 37)
    105–7
Huddart, Colour Sergeant Arthur, 92
Hutchinson, Bob, 15

If . . . (cartoon), (fig. 26) 93–5, 98,
    (fig. 31) 100, 102, 110, 111, 113,
    115 n21
Imperial War Museum, 59–60, 63,
    76, 82
In Which We Serve (film), 34–7, 42,
    48–9
Invincible, HMS, 131, 132
It's a Full Life in the Army (collage),
    65, (fig. 9) 66

Jagger, Charles Sargent, 72
Jak, 110
Jarman, Derek, x
Jenkins, Roy, 114
Jenkins, Simon, 16–17
Jones, Lieutenant Colonel Herbert H,
    8, (fig. 3) 23–6

Keane, John, 82
Kennard, Peter, 10, 65, (fig. 11) 67–9
Kent, John, 116 n29
Kissinger, Henry, 105–7
Kitson, Linda, (figs 6 and 7) 59–63,
    65, 74, 82, 83 n4
Kovic, Ron, 40

Langley, Bob, 123–4
Lawrence, Robert, 38–42
Leach, Admiral Sir Henry, 131
Lean, David, 34, 35, 42
Leeds Postcards, 74, 76, 115 n17
Lifeboat Ha! (sculpture), (fig. 15)
    73–4
Low, David, 85, 89, 97
Luce, Richard, 130

Mac, 86
McDonald, Ian, 69
McFadyen, Jock, 63–5, 77
maps, 8–9, 54, 81
Marines Show-Off Posters sent by The Sun, Ajax Bay (photograph), (fig. 2) 5
Massera, Admiral, 109
Medal of Dishonour (fine art), (fig. 12) 70
Memorial to HMS Sheffield (sculpture), 3, (fig. 1) 4
Memphis Belle (film), 48
Mendez, Costa, (fig. 21) 86, 109
Menem, Eduardo, 2
Menendez, General Mario Benjamin, 97
Middlebrook, Martin, 48
Milne, Alasdair, 29
Ministry of Defence, 1, 14, 29, 130, 134–5, 136, 137
montage, 10, (figs 9, 10 and 11) 65–9, (fig. 27) 95
Moore, Major Sir Jeremy, 15

Noon, Jeff, 118
Nott, John, 56, (fig. 21) 86, (fig. 39) 112, 130, 131, 136
novel, 3, 6, 10, 117–28

O'Connell, Surgeon Commander Morgan, 9, 78–9, 81
O-Zone (novel), 124
One Man's Falklands, 33
Osborne, John, ix
Out of this World (novel), 124

Peel, Michael, 10, 65, 67, 69
Pereira, Miguel, 46
Peron, General Juan Domingo, 52–3
photograph, 3, 5, 9, 10, 14, 16, 20, 56–7, 65–9, 81–2, 108–9, 133, 134, 135–6
Ponting, Clive, 29
Popadec, John, 69
post-traumatic stress disorder, 9, 41, 78–82
Powell, Michael, ix, 9, 37
Power, Maurice, 42
Press Association, 14–15

press, 3, 5, 7, 8, 10, 13–32, 43, 50–7, 58, 60, 63, 69, 74, 82, 84–115, 130–1, 133, 134–8
Pressburger, Emeric, ix, 9–10, 37
Preston, Peter, 15
Puttnam, David, 48
Pym, Francis, 108, 114 n4, 115 n18

QE2, 17, 60, 137

Rainbow Soldiers (novel), 120
Reach for the Sky (film), 34
Reagan, Ronald, 102–3, 108, 116 n23
Rejoice, Rejoice II (montage), (fig. 10) 67, 69
Resurrected (film), 9–10, 34, 43–6, 48–9, 118, 126
Robarts, Andy, 3
Rosoman, Leonard, 60
Rouco, Jose Iglesias, 51–2
Royal Marine Illustrators, 92
royalty, 4, 7–8, 13, 17, 18, 137
Rushdie, Salman, 117, 124

Sabat, (fig. 5) 53, 55, 108–9
Salway, Jon, 69
Sandle, Michael, 70, 72
Scarfe, Gerald, (fig. 21) 86, 102, 105, 115 n18
Schonfeld, Manfred, 51
Second World War, ix, 2, 4–5, 7, 11, 34–7, 48–9, 69, 76, 82, 84, 92, (fig. 28 and 30) 96–9, 102, 108, 119, 121–2, 127
Select Committee of the Ministry of Defence, 13–16, 28
Sgt. Ian McKay VC. Mount Longdon 11–12 June 1982 (painting), (fig. 17) 77
Shaw, Don, 28
Sheepsheds at Fitzroy – 2nd Battalion Scots Guards (drawing), (fig. 6) 61
Sheffield, HMS, 3–4, 22, 102, 105, 109, 135, 137, 115 n18
Simon's War, Simon's Peace, Simon's Triumph (documentary), 26–31
Sink the Belgrano (drama), 118
Smith, Tom, 9

South Atlantic Appeal Fund, 3, 38, 41, 70
South Atlantic Souvenirs, 74, 76, 94, (fig. 27) 95, 115 n17
Special Deliverance (novel), 120–1
Spycatcher, x, 29
Stark, Koo, 7
Steadman, Ralph, 9, 10, 97
Steel, David, 114
Stellman, Martin, 44
Stone, Oliver, 40
Strike Force Falklands (novels), 119–21
Suez, ix–x, 37, 118, 132
Summer Soldier (memoir), 42–3
Swansong (novel), 124–6
Swift, Graham, 124

Task Force, 1, 3, 10, 14, 17, 19–20, 22–3, 42, 59, 61, 64, 74, 76, 92, 102, (fig. 34) 103, (fig. 36) 106, 107, 112, 129–39
Tebbit, Norman, 107, 113
Thatcher, Margaret, ix, 2, 6–8, 29, 34, 37, 49, 56, 63, 65, (fig. 21) 86, 87, 89, (fig. 25) 93, 95, 97–8, 100, 102, (figs 34 and 36) 103–9, 110, 112 (fig. 40) 113, 127, 129, 134, 138
The Canberra's Return to Southampton (painting), (fig. 18) 76–8
The Dam Busters (film), 34
The Falklands Factor (drama), 28
The Falklands War: The Untold Story, 9
The Falklands Whale (novel), 124
The Fight for the Malvinas: The Argentine Forces in the Falklands War, 48
The Life and Death of Colonel Blimp (film), ix, 9–10, 37
The Little Platoon: Diplomacy and the Falklands Dispute, 10–11
The Monocled Mutineer (TV drama), 29, 37
The Rudolf Steiner Hairdressing Salon, SS Canberra (drawing) (fig. 7) 61–2
The Satanic Verses (novel), 117, 124

The Soldier (poem), 24
The Tin-Pot Foreign General and the Old Iron Woman (satire), 87
The Unnecessary War, 69
Theroux, Paul, 124
Timerman, Jacopo, 51
Tinker, Lieutenant David, 94
Tisdall, Sarah, 29
trade unions, 8, 13, 52, 112–13, 114, 138, 116 n30
Training on Hermes (photograph), 10
Trog, 86, 89
True Grit (film), 41
Tumbledown (TV drama), 9, 37–42, 44, 48–9, 118, 126

United Nations Organisation, 89, 92, (fig. 25) 93, 132
United States Latin America Policy, 102

Veronico Cruz (film), 46–7, 48–9
Vickers, 4, 5, 7
Victory Parade, 6
Vietnam, 34, 40, 42, 110, 112, 118, 126–7, 133
Viola, General Roberto, 51

Waite, Keith, 7, 88, 89, (fig. 23) 90, 112, 138, 115 n13
Walker, Rick, 94, 111
We Dive at Dawn (film), 34, 36
Webb, Sergeant John, R., 92
Weight, Angela, 60
Welcoming Cup of Tea at San Carlos Settlement (photograph), 9
Weston, Simon, (fig. 4) 26–8, 30
When the Fighting is Over: Tumbledown, a Personal Story (memoir), 38, 39–40
Williams, Philip, 42–6
Winward, Walter, 120–1
With Singing Hearts ... Throaty Roarings (painting), (fig. 8) 63–5
Wood, Charles, 37–42
Woodward, Rear Admiral Sandy, 16, 20, 88, 100, 136–7
Woundings (drama), 118
Wright, Peter, 29

Zec, 98